Pursuing Legacy

Principles for an Influential Career & Impactful Life

I0142429

Porscha R. Jackson, PhD

Published in the United States of America by

Paisley Publishing, Houston, TX

Paperback ISBN: 978-0-692-72481-1

Ebook ISBN: 978-1-5323-0711-9

Cover Design: Andrew McCray

DEDICATION

To the memories of Alma Ford, Nancy Rollins, and Otis Rollins, Sr. The most kind, loving, giving, and selfless people who exemplified true humanity. I was blessed to have had you in my life in the capacity of grandmother, aunt, and uncle. I am forever grateful for your support of me and your life and legacy.

CONTENTS

ACKNOWLEDGMENTS

In all thy ways acknowledge Him and He will direct thy paths. Proverbs 3:6

Therefore, as always a special thanks to God, for whom I move and have my being. Secondly, I would like to acknowledge my mom and the rest of my family and friends for all of their continuous support.

I would like to express my sincere gratitude to two people who encouraged me to write this book, one knowingly and the other unknowingly. Roughly about four or five years ago, I was leaving a New Year's celebration at my church. As I was approaching the door to leave, a man approached me and began to speak to me, he was really trying to make a pass, but in his conversation made a profound statement. In talking about my nonprofit organization and my recent decision to pursue a doctorate, he said "I can see you being an author." Immediately, in my mind I dismissed it but before I opened my mouth, something said 'don't shoot it down, don't limit yourself because of the source'. So I responded "ok, maybe". Wow, now I thank him because he put the initial thought in my mind that I could be an author.

The other person I would like to thank is Dr. Lisa Baumgartner, who served on my dissertation committee. I was not even remotely thinking about writing a book at the time of my dissertation, let alone thinking this would be the topic for my first book. I remember in her office, she was helping me understand narrative analysis and she suggested I write a book after I completed my dissertation. She even went as far as giving me an example of someone who had done it and that person has made significant strides in the academic world. For her to think and have faith in my work, was amazing and humbling. Dr. Baumgartner, I will never forget your act of kindness and your belief in my ability.

Lastly, I must acknowledge the families who shared their stories with me so freely.

i

Pursuing Legacy

INTRODUCTION

The fascination with legacy or what one will leave for future generations starts as part of a self-reflection near middle-age. Dan P. McAdams explained a stage in one's life-span that deals with generativity. Generativity is a term coined by Erik Erikson that describes a person's concern with guiding and providing for the next generation for the progression of society. I argue it may not be a specific age but perhaps a stage in life after great turning points and terrifying experiences, as scholar Ernest Becker described in his theory of terror management. Whatever the circumstance, I'm sure we can all agree, if we are fortunate to live long enough, we will all at some point have thoughts of how we will be remembered and the legacy we will leave.

So what is legacy and what does it really mean in terms of careers and family? Well that is the purpose of this book and will be answered through the various stories and information shared. Objectively, legacy is defined by Webster as a handed down heritage or a bequest. But as you think about it and will read in this book, it is more than just heritage, but a greater multitude of things consisting of identity, confidence, knowledge, behavior, and resources that are inbred, maintained, practiced, and told through our very being of existence, consciously and subconsciously.

The Bible addresses legacy, specifically in Proverbs 13:22, when it states we are to leave something for our children's children. So it is inevitable as McAdams pointed out, we will come to a point in life where the stage of generativity will surface. I suggest legacy is heavily intertwined with our career choices and social and communal activities. Therefore, with this book, I present if we begin to think about the legacy we will leave as we approach our career decisions, the ways we approach our jobs and careers will be more purposeful and thus a positive fulfillment that succeeds throughout generations.

What we must begin to understand is the reactions, feelings, and discussions about our jobs are infectious. If a job keeps you away from your family, then your children who look up to you may shy away from that career because they have a negative memory of it keeping away a person with whom they wanted to spend more time. The same occurs with our social decisions, as authors Besemer and Farrington indicated an intergenerational transfer of social behavior from parents to children. Besemer and Farrington exemplify their statement with the observations children make of their parents' experiences in and out of jail. The scholars acknowledge these observations have a subconscious effect on the limitations and lowered expectations of children who will follow in the modeled footsteps because they were shown no other way. So when you look at it from this angle, it is no wonder why 70% percent of children with incarcerated parents will follow in their parents' footsteps.

This is sad, but it does not have to be, we can change this outcome. Legacies can be positive and negative. There are a multitude of family businesses that are generational because of someone's admiration of a family member or involvement in the family businesses at a young age. From this involvement, they sought to model that behavior and worked hard to provide for their family or joined in the business to elevate the family name. This is also true for families without business ownership, who have built a legacy from their intergenerational careers, such as: teaching, farming, military service, and law enforcement, to name a few, and have managed to have their children follow in their career footsteps to maintain this career legacy.

This is where my expertise comes into play. I am a researcher with a focus on career legacies, especially those maintained by families. In fact, this book is a continuation of the years of research I have done in this area for academic purposes. The legacies, careers, and family business are all intertwined here to produce the career stories on family career legacy. To fully understand, we must take it back to the root of family and career.

Robert Chope, a prolific scholar in the area of familial influence on careers, talked about the origin of careers in family and how it was expected centuries ago that once of age, a child would enter and take on the same occupation as his father. Think about it, farmers, preachers, were all generational careers. It wasn't until the mid-20th century when it became more common for children to go away to college and as a result would move to more metropolitan cities for job opportunities not available in the small towns of origin. Historically speaking, in the development of a nation, families typically followed in the same career path of their family members because as towns expanded into larger cities, people tried to stay near family. However, as time progressed and resources dispersed, individuals left their hometowns for better career opportunities. Chope discovered, in this departure, people became less happy and began to rely on the lessons taught by their family for career survival. In turn, this allowed learning about the family characteristics and discovering what could be learned from family histories, successes, and failures important to career decision making. As such, family expectations put pressure to positively affect how people decided what they should do with their lives.

When looking at the family career legacy from the point of family business, the pressure from family expectations becomes essentially important when you consider the statistics of family business and its role in the United States economy. In the United States, family businesses are at the heart of entrepreneurship with approximately 10.8 million family businesses accounting for 59% of the country's gross domestic product (GDP), which equates to $5.5 trillion and the employment of 77 million people (58% of the workforce).

I am not suggesting a career legacy is only expressed through family business. I am merely suggesting involvement in family business is the most common way of experiencing career legacy and through the study of the family businesses, the concept is easier to conceive and understand. Therefore, this book will delve into what it means to create and maintain a career legacy through the individual, real-life career stories of members involved in their family businesses. What you will learn from a look at these six family career legacies are the elements of establishing and maintaining a legacy. We will review in the chapters of this book how each person or family member strived to leave their own legacy as an inclusion or branch, if you will, to the overall family legacy. A straw in a stack of hay to say the least.

What I am proposing to you is when you begin to approach your career with the thought of leaving a legacy, it will be a step in changing how you approach your future. You must realize the future development of yourself can have a long-lasting positive reflection on your children, future generations, community, and society as a whole.

I ask you to read each chapter and learn from these families' lived experiences and the reflection notes at the end of each chapter as suggestions and nuggets to help you think of your job/career as something more than an occupation or a paycheck. Please grasp that as an employee you are spending your time for the exchange of payment, yes, but it's more than that. Make it worth more…you owe it to the next generation to create a better society and way of life. You see, you never get time back, and as cliché as it is, life is short, so make it worthwhile, make it work for you, and make an impact.

Enjoy the journey these stories will take you on and I hope this book sparks a revelation in how you can pursue your career with legacy in mind.

Here are some definitions of terms that will be frequently used in this book and will be helpful when reading.

1. Career: individually perceived sequence of attitudes & behaviors associated with work-related experiences and activities over the span of the person's life
2. Career identity: identity where others connect their own aspirations, motivations, skillsets, and abilities to acceptable career roles
3. Family business: a business owned and operated by members of a family with the intention of the family maintaining majority control
4. Family career legacy: conglomeration of associated career experiences, reputations, and behaviors shared and passed on to and through generations that construct and maintain a collective identity
5. Generative thinking: a process of thinking to help future generations
6. Generativity: a psychological construct that involves leaving a legacy through the linkage of past and future experiences and encompassing the creation, maintenance, and preservation
7. Intergenerational careers: identical careers held by family members of different generations
8. Job: an occupational and/or employment position
9. Legacy: anything, mainly intangible items or concepts that are handed down from one generation to the next generation

10. Social identity: an identity as a result of one's membership or association with a social group or status

Pursuing Legacy

CHAPTER 1

"The home is the ultimate career. All other careers exist for
one purpose, and that is to support the ultimate career."
--C.S. Lewis

In family career legacies, the career is the focal point of the legacy. This
career, whether family business oriented or not, sets the precedence of
what is means to be a member of that family. The career becomes the
carrier of family values, passions, resources, business networks,
accomplishments, reputation, and even identity. Essentially, it creates
patterns for a way of living.

For instance, in earlier centuries it was understood the career your
father had, was the career you would have, it was automatically
expected that you would follow in your father's footsteps.
Additionally, children were expected to participate and work to
contribute to the maintenance of the household. This was a time
before the child labor law but it would be remiss to ignore that plenty
of children worked to help their father and mother with their jobs and
the family business, after this law was passed. Therefore, the family
values and ethics became engrained into the future generations of what
it meant to be a member of that particular family because as a child,
you were an extension of the working parent and expected to uphold
the parent's reputation.

To take it a step further, early American families received their last
names due to their profession, such as: Baker, Farmer, Taylor, etc.

Ever wonder why Smith is the most popular American last name? Because to be a goldsmith, blacksmith, and any other type were some of the most popular professions and through the years, their profession was shortened into the last name of Smith. Therefore, your family name spoke volumes of who you were and what you would be, because it was a direct indication of your profession. Moreover, your profession dictated your social status and ultimately, the lifestyle for you and your children.

It was not until the industrialization era where children began to leave the home in greater volumes, in hopes to find employment in other cities and/or attend college, which afforded them better employment opportunities in larger metropolitan cities. In their departures, their family reputations followed them, often opening doors for some, as they relied on their family foundation of values and learned skills to become successful. As such, this new generation of workers would send funds back to their homes to assist their parental household or send for their families to join them in their new environment.

In this first chapter, I introduce the concept of the home as the ultimate career and how it creates a legacy through the story of the Whitney family.[1] This family's career legacy will open your eyes to the importance of the familial influence on career decisions and how patterns, environment, community, and society, collectively, can form legacies that impact future generations.

The Whitney Family: Legacy of Beauty

The career legacy of the Whitney family is one rich in beautiful history that stretches over 100 years. It is a testament that from a dark heritage filled with oppression, segregation, and discrimination, a sense

---

[1] Due to University Institutional Review Board protocol where this research was approved, the names of all the participants for this book and any direct identifying information, such as their locations, business names, etc. have been assigned pseudonyms to uphold the integrity of the conducted research.

Figure 1: Whitney Family Tree

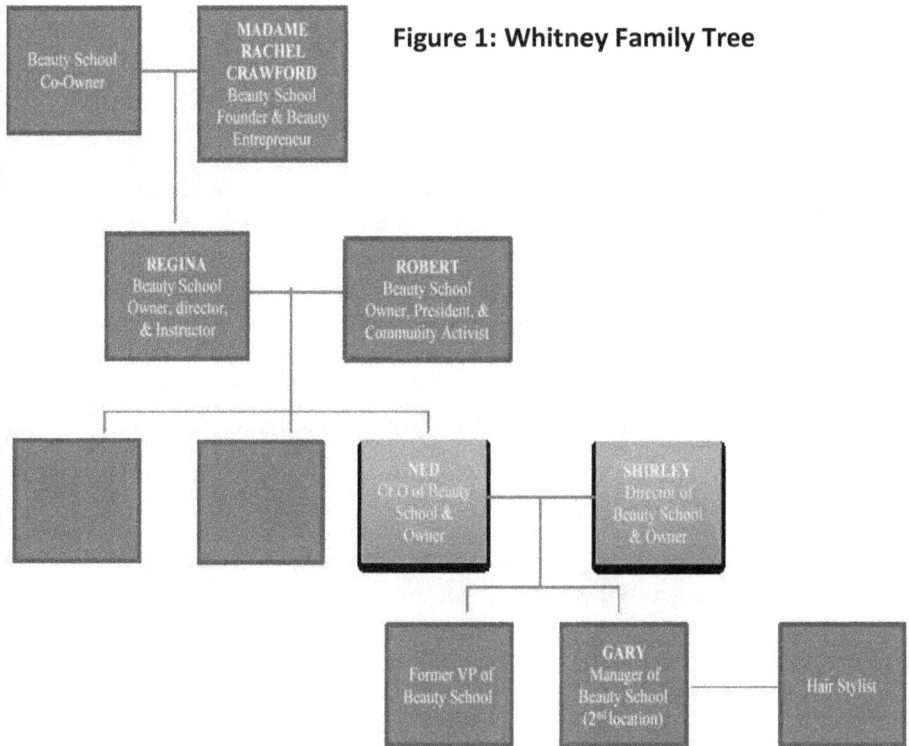

of pride, opportunity, privilege, and community can emerge for the dawning of a new legacy. This legacy spawned from the notorious career of pioneer, Madame C.J. Walker, the first Black millionaire, who was a mentor to the matriarch and founder of the Whitney family career legacy, Madame Rachel Crawford. Madame Crawford's leadership in the Whitney's story has been frequently told and researched. The evolution of this family career legacy (Figure 1) has received recognition as a staple in the Black Harrison City community. In fact, their family history is the subject of a book on the beauty industry in the Jim Crow era.

The Whitney family consists of four generations in the beauty industry through the manufacturing and production of Black hair care products, hair styling, and the establishment and maintenance of a beauty school. The family career legacy begins with the entrepreneurial career of Madame Rachel Crawford which began in the early 1900's.

Her only daughter, Regina and son-in-law Robert, served as the second generation establishing one of the first beauty schools for Blacks during the Jim Crow era of segregation in Harrison and elevating the school to a staple of opportunity in the Harrison Black community and the state. Groomed to take over the reign from his father, Ned and his wife Shirley began their succession in 1969 as the third generation to run the family business. The family business, which now consists of multiple locations of Crawford Beauty School in Harrison, have ushered in the fourth generation of Ned and Shirley's son, Gary, to take the business past its centennial and well into the 21st century. This family career legacy is told from the perspective of the third generation, Ned and Shirley, coupled with historic accounts as documented through books and articles of the family's history.

Legacy History

The early decades of the 20th century in America proved to be some of the prominent times for careers and occupations for African American women in the beauty industry. It provided a career alternative away from traditional laborious jobs in the fields, factories, and domestic work during a time when racial segregation was at its peak. A particular point in time referred to as the Jim Crow era, which spanned from the late 1800's to the mid 1960's. The Jim Crow laws enacted racial segregation stated as 'separate but equal', meaning that all public facilities, including restrooms, restaurants, movie theaters, stores, schools, housing, and even areas of town in Southern states had designations as 'White only' or 'Colored only'. However, though these facilities were separate, they were not equal, with establishments for Blacks being inferior to those of Whites. This era was the result of White supremacy acts that created an unequal society.

During these times, the only businesses that offered specific needs for Blacks without White competition were beauty salons, barbershops, photographers, and funeral homes. Therefore beauticians and cosmetology teachers and students found their niche as they began to study and service Black women, who were eager to patronize establishments that welcomed them. Black cosmetology schools and beauticians were able to succeed because women of color held their personal appearance in high regard. Blackwelder, a historian, stated "For black women, hair matters embody one's identity, beauty, power, and consciousness". Thus, there became an influx of licensed beauticians who achieved a social status higher than the domestic service but lower than school teachers, who at that time were regarded as having legitimate and lucrative professions. The expansion of the Black beauty industry flourished as many women traveled throughout the nation to attend cosmetology schools, in search of job skills and employment upon completion.

The history of Crawford Beauty School enfolds several stories: a business history, a family history, urban history, African American history, and gender history. It is a history of ordinary people whose aspirations and accomplishments through the Jim Crow era speak both to the injustices of racial discrimination and to the resilience of African Americans' determination to make good in a world that conspired against them.

First Generation

In 1915, when most Black businesses were barbershops, grocery stores, restaurants and delivery services, Madame Rachel Crawford, a student of beauty pioneer and mogul Madame C.J. Walker, started manufacturing her own hair products and teaching hairdressing and beauty care to Black in-home clients via horse and buggy in the south. Two years later, Madame Crawford settled in Harrison and established a presence through the manufacturing and selling of her hair and beauty products and an established training program. After such, according to her family, she established the first beauty salon in the state. Located in Marlon County and then replicated in Harrison, this salon became and is still known as Crawford Beauty School, a full-service cosmetology school. A few years later, Madame Crawford would move to Illinois during the Great Migration (a time period in America where southern Blacks moved to northern cities to escape the injustices of the south and for better job opportunities) to expand her career, where she owned and operated a beauty school and continued the manufacturing of her cosmetic products until her death in 1934.

Second Generation

While in Illinois, Madame Crawford incorporated her young daughter, Regina into the business, teaching her hair styling techniques, product formulas and processes, and promoting her to vice president and instructor, all before she graduated from high school. To ensure their quality of their products and service and perpetuate their values and practices, the mother and daughter team organized a formal association to ensure standardized and ownership approved treatment methods, that they called "The Whitney Way is the Right Way". This way would later be adopted by others in the beauty industry and become part of a movement that would lead to a professional association to progress their business and encourage spirituality and prosperity of its members.

A licensed beautician, Regina continued to run the business with her mother, who slowly began to delegate major responsibilities to her daughter and student, Robert Whitney. Robert's business sense and great teaching and hairdressing skills, ushered him as manager of business operations; after marrying Regina, the two succeeded Madame Crawford as the second generation. Now in charge of the finance and operations, Robert brought in his sister to help with running the salon and her husband to assist with the manufacturing.

Under the second generation, the business grew in all facets. As heirs to the business after Madame Crawford's death, Robert and Regina left the Illinois operation in the hands of his relatives as a means of financial support. The couple then sought for greater opportunity for the business and moved to Harrison and reestablished Crawford Beauty School, in physical form, in a thriving area of the city for Blacks in 1935. The population in the 1930's for Harrison Blacks was growing, making it the largest in the Southwest. The Black community had leading newspapers and publications which promoted opportunity to its readers. Blacks in this city were considered enterprising and were committed to education.

Settling into Harrison, the Whitney's began to revive Crawford Beauty School. Their hard work and determination under Robert's vision propelled Crawford Beauty School to the largest Black beauty school in the south with a student population representative of various parts of the country and eager for the opportunity of education, skill development, and employment. Regina served as manager, instructor, director, and vice president, often serving as a mother figure to the out-of-town students who stayed in the school's dormitories. Her nurturing spirit helped with the personal development of the young women.

Robert served as president guiding and growing the business in the community; in addition to the school, they also had three beauty salons. As business prospered, so did his community involvement. As the school progressed, Robert began to make several business investments in the stock market and in oil leases, which led him to be recognized as a pillar in the community and a viable member of the Black middle class. He owned rental properties and was given the award as the Bronze Mayor. He had leadership in local, state, and national beauty industry professional organizations. He also joined the Negro Chamber of Commerce and Phi Beta Sigma, and other groups that promoted African American business success, civility in Harrison, and community development. His involvement gained him community-wide respect and his leadership and involvement in politics helped to break racial barriers in Harrison. He even began to seek popularity for his business investments. Through all his various civic involvement and activities, Robert never neglected his role in the school and led the school into success into the 1960's, helping to shape lives of young Black women through a shot at a lucrative career. His management of the school made it one of the most profitable businesses in Harrison, which added to the percentage of the overall sales and third largest Black business groups in Black Harrison.

Described as frugal with a generous heart, Robert pledged funds and led fundraising efforts for the establishment of YMCA activities to better the Black community. He was a member and head of many related beauty professional organizations. In fact his civic leadership and community involvement led to several milestones in the Harrison Black community, beauty industry, and the City of Harrison in general. For example, Robert had gained significant respect that the State Board of Cosmetology agreed to hold its licensing examination at the school instead of at the state capitol, in order to save its students funds in traveling to the capital city to take the examination. Additionally,

7

Robert worked with the City-Wide Beauticians Association which led to change in state policies and standards and a limit of licensing fees. He united beauty school owners of various races against a bond change. One significant example is his involvement led to the appointment of the first shop inspector of color in the state, in which he wrote Governor Ford "is gratifying not only to the beauty shop owners and operators, but, is a recognition to over one million disfranchised people who enjoy but little of the full citizenship and economic strength of this great state". Because of his civic leadership and financial position, White Harrison residents would call on his assistance for racial change.

Robert used the standards set by his mother-in-law in the industry to propel race relations and draw attention to politics surrounding the industry and business. He even was instrumental in encouraging Blacks to vote and ending segregation of Harrison golf courses in the 1950's, which jumpstarted started a city-wide desegregation. Robert accomplished a lot in his 35 year career at Crawford Beauty School in Harrison. His legacy was honored for his business achievement and civic leadership of moving Whites and Blacks beyond the Jim Crow era.

Together, Robert and Regina took Madame Crawford's legacy and made it a lasting enterprise, graduating 100 to 200 students a year. In fact, from 1935 to the 1970's, the couple was accredited for preparing 25,000 cosmetologists for the workforce. Blackwelder stated "Whitney's tutelage made paths for succeeding generations of African Americans who, in the face of seemingly overwhelming odds, freed themselves from a life of service to Whites and advanced into dignified economic independence through skills that they and their clients valued". A career legacy that has positioned the third generation for success, as Madame Crawford did for the second generation.

Third Generation

The third generation of the Whitney family career legacy consists of Ned and Shirley, the son and daughter-in-law of Robert and Regina.

Ironically, on Juneteenth, I interviewed Ned and Shirley at their school, which is now located in a plaza in a historical area of Harrison known for its high Black population. This location, though in place many years, is now adjacent from the city's Martin Luther King, Jr. memorial statue.

I became knowledgeable of the Whitney's family career legacy two ways. A few years prior, I had watched a show that focused on the Crawford Beauty School and its students and at that time, I became aware of the family business and its longevity in the community. Secondly, when speaking with a colleague about my research topic, they suggested this family as potential participants because of their awareness of the legacy and the criteria of my study. Therefore, I called the school to schedule an interview with Shirley. When I called the following week as a reminder to Shirley of our appointment the following day, I spoke with Ned and was able to secure an interview with him as well.

The next day, I arrived at the school nearly 30 minutes after its opening to find two students at their stations, quietly styling mannequin heads, a man behind the desk speaking on the phone, and a woman stocking a cabinet behind the desk. As I waited to be helped, I noticed how large the space was. There were several student work stations, about four shampoo bowls in the back left corner, a classroom in the center of the back of the facility, and to my very right a hallway that led to offices and other rooms. The walls had typical beauty school pictures of hairstyles, except one which had a collage of articles and pictures documenting the school's proud historic moments.

The man behind the desk nudges the woman stocking to assist me. She, dressed casually with a smock, asks how she can help me. I explain and she invites me to sit as she gets Shirley for me. While I'm sitting, the man who was taking the phone call comes from behind the desk and greets me. He is a medium built man, who appeared in his 60's, charmingly introduces himself and states that he was the one who spoke to me when I called to schedule the interviews. He tells me how great it is to put a face to a name and then introduces me to his wife as she enters the waiting area. Shirley is a woman of medium-build with glasses and a conservative, tightly curled bob with blonde highlights. I follow her back to a spacious room that contains three to four desks and a copier and our interview begins. Before the recorder starts, she warns me she does not have much time as she has to prepare for a conference call and she can only allot 30 minutes for the interview. Her answers reflect her haste, so we began.

SHIRLEY'S STORY

As an in-law, married into the family legacy, Shirley first describes her family-of-origin.

EXISTENCE OF CAREER INFLUENCES AND ROLE MODELS

I'm from a family of four kids, my dad was adamant to all of us that we were going to go to college after high school and actually every one of us did get our college degree because of my dad's strong influence on our lives...Well I have to say both my mother and father. Because they were a strong inspiration in my life and they supported things I wanted to do. I think they reared us very good, because we're all successful. Um the legends would be, uh my husband's grandmother who started the school in 1915. My husband's grandmother, as I said, Madame Rachel Crawford, that's where the name Crawford Beauty School comes from. It's his mother's mother, uh, she started the school back in 1915 on horse and buggy. She would go to homes teaching people how to do hair cause back then there was no such thing as a beauty school, back in her day. And so eventually my father-in-law and mother-in-law took over the business and actually Crawford Beauty School was one of the first licensed beauty schools in the state, maybe in the United States.

[It was actually] my father-in-law [who] encouraged me to get my cosmetology license once I got married and I was really shocked because I had no desire to do hair or be in the hair business. But I respected him a lot and did what he asked me to do and here I am now 45 years later.

FAMILY VALUES

The values are to be successful to do what you want to do in a positive way and we encourage my son to be successful even though he's smart...sometimes I think he's smarter than me and my husband. (laughs) Interactions? Um just encourage each other, don't forget you have a mother and father, you have your children and your children are to um treat you as you treated us and they'll see that coming from you, they'll observe that.

PRESSURE & SUPPORT

There was no pushing me to go in one direction, the pushing was 'you are going to go college!' I feel absolutely no pressure. We're all individuals, we're in different careers and we encourage and support each other in what we do but no pressure.

Regarding the support received from her family, she adds
Just verbally encouraging me, ah both my mom and dad very good parents. Well my mom and dad and my sisters and my brother had no idea that I would change careers after I finished college. They wanted me to be what I wanted to be and I wanted to be a teacher, so they encouraged me to get my credentials to do that.

MAKING MEANING OF CAREER EXPERIENCES

Uh the very first job I had, I was probably, uh, trying to think how old I was... I was cleaning houses, I was in school but on Saturday I would go and clean houses because I wanted my own money. And I made like $5 a day (laughs) which to me was a lot of money. And so that was my first job and I was and that was while I was in junior high school, I would do that. And after that, um I went to school, college, and I started working at the United States Post Office and actually I worked at the post office and went to college at the same time. I finished college in four years, which people don't do that anymore. They take their time, but you know I was determined to do what I wanted to do. The reason I wanted to work in the post office, I wanted my own car and I was able to do that, get my car. To me it was really awesome that I could go to school and work in a post office and finished school on time, college. And then from there I finished college and quit the post office and I got married and actually got married the week before I graduated from college.

The week after I graduated college, I was preparing myself to get a job in a high school to teach French and that's when my father-in-law encouraged me to take the course. So I took the course, so once I took the course, he purchased a second school and made me the manager at 23 years old. And then, God the students were not like they are today. Back then, because I don't know at 23 there were times I had to go in the stock room and cry, but I never let anybody see me cry because I had to have this tough image to manage the school. So here I am, like I said 45 years later. When I made this career decision...the impact was going to be good because I was going to be involved in business.

Shirley's demeanor immediately changes, she sits upright, begins to smile and feel more comfortable.

I love helping people. Our students have so many issues and one of my main functions as director of Crawford Beauty School is to give them ideas and recommend them to go and see certain agencies to help them if they have drug problems and stuff like that, uh but my main, the thing I love most about this job is I love helping students.

CONTINUING THE LEGACY

Well I hope the next generation will realize that if a student is having issues that's preventing them from trying to finish a course, do everything in your power to help and encourage them and let them know they can be successful in this field but they have to deal with the personal problems first.

So hopefully, um I can leave my image to the next generation in the fact that I'm known for helping people. Success is accomplishing what you want to do. If I could talk about it in terms of this particular career, uh come to school, get your license, go work in a salon, and start making a lot of money as my daughter-in-law does right now.

As the interview with Shirley ends, Ned comes into the office area and she yells, "It's your turn!" He then contemplates whether or not he wants to do the interview, stating that he does not do well in interviews. Shirley then says, "This is YOUR family!" and he sits down at the desk and our interview begins.

NED'S STORY

FAMILY BEGINNINGS

You know its interesting cause growing up, my mother and father growing up ran this business as I was a kid growing up and working with them and working with my dad, my ambition was to be involved with the business, not owning it, but being involved because that's all I knew. Yes, as long as I can remember, I'm tagging along with him. My brother and I, um, going to school to clean up and do whatever, I would say five, six years old. Well working with them, being around the business, I visually saw what the business was and what it did of course in the early days as I was a child.

Ned then recounted some of the jobs he had as a child and other things that stood out to him in childhood.

The manufacturing side of the business, producing the product which was the original inception of the business and that was an integral part of the business side that I knew nothing about, didn't understand as a child, uh but the manufacturing of the actual product as a child, I assisted as a little helper. Cleanup guy whatever and basically we produced the product, took it to the school, sold it, and used it.

Oh well, um my grandmother, Rachel Crawford, better known as Madame Crawford. She learned her art uh by trial and error and some of it was under the direction of CJ Walker and she was able to learn the foundationals [sic] that CJ Walker had and she set out on her own to do her own thing and she developed Madame Crawford's beauty products. From there my mother and father took over and continued the same operation and began the school teaching aspect when it was in the State in 1935.

Well you know as a child, I'm outside in the manufacturing entry plant, which was outside behind the home, as a child and I'm out there every two days, three days a week helping my dad. And my brother and I out there, helping my dad manufacture products, um becoming junior high or middle school kid continued that same course in high school, began to work jobs outside of the family business, uh grocery store, sacking groceries or whatever. And then and uh I remember at age 15, 16 at the Shamrock Hotel for a period of time. I was a sheltered type of child growing up.

EXISTENCE OF CAREER INFLUENCES AND ROLE MODELS

My dad only... [my parents]they were self-taught, uh in the business world. Um and they basically, I think their philosophy, I never knew this, was to self-teach any sibling that wanted to follow in their footstep in the business. Very hard business, very tough, very hard work, and they were very hard workers. My dad and both, both, my dad and my mom, my mom was low keyed and reserved and very supportive. Uh she was a mom and my dad was more forceful and more vigorous and uh "you can do it" and it didn't matter what it was. "You not only can do it but you will do it". You know my dad, being a member of a major association during his tenure, um as an owner of a small business and had friends of real estate and doctors and lawyers and printers and suppliers and manufacturers and all the people. I tagged along with him, to be around him, he would take me along quite a bit, my dad would be that person.

FAMILY VALUES

Interaction rules, interesting question, family interaction rules…well a lot of things that old school teachers are always trying, um you know things my mom would say, "stay true to yourself" or I think she would say things like that. A lot of things she would say I wouldn't remember or understand. My dad would though, I call them innuendos, back then, um work ethics little things like that, "if a man doesn't work he'll steal". Um a lot of work ethics continuing 'not to be lazy, get up in the morning, feel proud to be'.

Oh here is a little quick story and hopefully we can end on this one. After school in junior high school and high school, my immediate task was to leave school and go right to work. At that time 15, 16 years old, um my job was to clean the building up at the school at that time in the afternoon, 2:30, 3:00. One day my job was to go outside and wash the windows. The school had huge plate-glass windows out front. I um did not want to go outside and wash the windows. My ego said "don't do that cause your friends are going to pass and see you", was I ashamed? Probably. So the job was to go out and wash the windows, my dad found me in the back hiding and says "why aren't you doing what I asked?" I said "dad my friends might pass by". He said "come on" and, he was a shirt and tie type of guy, and he rolled up his sleeves and we got the bucket and sponge and things and uh we went outside. He made me go out and wash the windows together and uh his slogan or his implantation for me in my mind was "always remember you have windows to wash and your friends riding by have no windows". And that instilled in me something that I always remembered because it was a very true statement cause here I am taking care of a business that's family owned and my friends are riding and have no business or nothing. So I've always remembered that; I've passed that along.

PRESSURE & SUPPORT

I don't know if they [my parents] really wanted us, my brothers and sister, to pursue this career till we got older. Knowing how hard they worked and struggled through the days from post-depression to the 50's to the early 60's, so um as far as education wise, we continued in our elementary education, high school education, and on to college. But nothing being pushed towards any particular career and particular degree. (In response to a later question, Carl stated the opposite after he agreed to succeed his father with the business.) I was thrust into becoming involved with anything that had anything to do with the beauty industry, from national associations to local groups, being involved and being aware of what people think and what people do.

This is a pattern that was done by his father when he was president of the school and now this is something that his son, Gary, is now involved. Regarding the support received from his family, he declared "they were there 100,000%, so anything I wanted and needed I got within reason. Very much hands on all the time".

MAKING MEANING OF CAREER EXPERIENCES

After high school, of course um, off to college and of course probably had some menial temporary type jobs. Then I went into as an accountant or a junior accountant at the medical center here in Harrison at age 20, 21. I was there for about a year and a half to two years and then got married, of course, and after I got married my dad said 'you know it's time for you to take over the business'. All the time within all these junctures I'm working with the business at some point and not with the business, I'm working with my dad and his real estate investments and that's from cleaning apartments to painting to whatever else. I'm a busy person cutting grass and whatever else.

I felt, you know, once I got my footing, my dad turned the business over to us, unto me. I felt I was ready to conquer anything within the business. I had the resources, the exposure to the other schools around the state, um and I had peers who would nurture me in areas and I was able to pick up the phone and call someone in other cities or wherever they were. School owners, such as myself for information and advice needed beyond my dad's retirement…He was ready to go.

In reflecting on why this particular career appeals to him, he responded,

Ah it's the joy of seeing young people who don't know where their lives are going, have aspirations to achieve something.

Uh it's very difficult and now a days this century to take a, um a young person and really mold them to becoming a professional in the cosmetology business. It's just so much more involved from being an artist and hair designing and hair sculpturing or perming or coloring or cutting. It's so much more involved in the business than just the artistry itself, it takes the whole person and to most schools, in fact I know of no schools that can actually mold a person in all those phases.

It has to come from within and so my challenge has become limited in today's society as to the types of individuals we receive to try to make them...we can make them work ready, we can supply them to the workforce but the survival ratio is a lot tougher now than it was 10-20 years ago, when his father was in charge. The accomplishment that was done for a little, small mom pop business like we are, I feel are astronomical because being the first, um cosmetology school in the State of any color ownership, one of the first in 1935, um being third generation now and fourth generation being in the business and knowing that Madame Crawford started in 1915 and the institution is still surviving in 2014, we're 99 years, is quite an accomplishment.

SENSE OF BELONGING AND COMMUNITY

Being an educational institution our goal was to train people to become professionals and go out into the work world and survive. Um so after completion of that training and going out in the work world, we followed up with things such as our own person, our own company alumni association which is a very active, integral part of the graduates continuing their act, their studies.

PIVOTAL AND TURNING POINT EXPERIENCES IN CAREER

Oh well the Vietnam War, I was, I had gotten my papers to be inducted right after I got married. Um and right after that our first child was coming and I'm getting something that says "report" and I did not want to report and I was very afraid. I was a sheltered type of child growing up and had um food water and a roof over my head and had no idea what military life was about and had no idea what the Vietnam War was about...a bunch of people fighting over in another land. So uh that was a very deep challenge to me, I was not selected to go and I pushed forward to stay in town and continue to build the business.

In the year 2014 as we are now, the overall sustainability of a business like this, a small mom and pop type business is extremely difficult to operate. The pressures of the government, the pressures of big educational institutions, they gobble up the large resources that are available even to small schools, makes it difficult to sustain. You have to sometimes, instead of expand, we're in expanding mode, which is something that I want to do, but we're more or less in a slowdown mode or a scaling down mode at this point in 2014. Next year who knows?

CONTINUANCE OF THE LEGACY

Well there is only one really that aspires to be better than my dad or myself and that's my son, Gary and he will be and he is becoming that. Of course my wife, Shirley and I took over in 1971. I believe and uh its third generation. I would think that my son, Gary, being involved in the business and actually managing our second location right now currently, and he's at that capacity 100% right now, and it's his total responsibility to make that institution survive so that would be the one, Gary.

I think his challenge is to surpass anything we've ever accomplished. Um from being involved in national associations to being elected to this office and having traveled all over the United States to visiting other schools across the country to being involved in a lot of local activities and fundraisers and some degree of philanthropy, uh giving back to community, community involvement being on the boards of YMCA, and the women's home, etc. etc. My son Gary, he wants to surpass all that and we're an inspiration to him and the things that we've done.

Here the pattern of Robert's and Ned's involvement in the community has been observed by Gary and is testament to following in the footsteps of his father and grandfather and associating the involvement with these organizations as part of his career identity and what it means to be president of the school.

He continues,

Well I hope to leave for my siblings or my two sons, one is totally involved in the business the others have moved on at this point but that's okay. The ability to understand that you have to keep up with this business is not something you can just sit aside and let someone else run it. You have to be hands on, you have to understand every avenue of how it works, and he [Gary] knows that, he understands that and if he continues then he'll be successful.

What was interesting is though Ned expressed some reservations in doing the interview, he was honored to have someone to research his family career legacy. His face lit-up when he told me stories, especially those of his father. After the interview, he spent five to ten minutes telling me where to find additional resources to learn more about his family and how he wanted to find a way to teach current students the history behind the school, in order for them to fully understand the purpose of Crawford Beauty School.

Chapter Summary

The Whitney family has a rich family career legacy demonstrative of how each generation has a role in its continuance. Each generation took a leadership role in progressing the family business by getting the next generation involved at a young age and providing a more structured and viable income opportunity. What I admire about this family was the willingness of their spouses to contribute to the legacy and play a significant role in the continuation of the family business. In summary, the Whitneys teach us the following about the creation and maintenance of a family career legacy.

1. Create positive career patterns.
   a. Recognize that you have the power to create a pattern in how your children and others will follow into your footsteps based on the example, support, and resources you provide.
2. Use the family business as a leverage to make a greater communal impact.
   a. Understand the family legacy must exist outside of the family to perpetuate its story and values.
   b. Aligning your passion with social responsibility to eradicate social injustices is a way to not only serve your community but to advance your profession and develop more clientele.
   c. Think about issues in your environment you would like to change as motivation, like Robert did with the civil rights issues in Harrison.
3. Contribute to the family career legacy your personal legacy.
   a. Using the family career legacy can help to propel your personal legacy, which can become a branch in the family legacy.
   b. Use the business to provide an even greater way of life for future generations and make it easier for them to continue the legacy. This will help to create the positive patterns as discussed in number 1.

4. Include children and other family members in the business.
   a. Family values and ethics are perpetuated through the family business and careers by involving them. This involvement demonstrates the values and belief system that is taught. And it also demonstrates teamwork.

CHAPTER 2

"Your story is the greatest legacy that you will leave to your friends. Its's the longest-lasting legacy you will leave to your heirs." --Steve Saint

When we consider our legacy and what it entails, we must understand the importance of the stories we tell and how we live out these stories in our daily interactions. The messages we receive from our family build the foundation of our perspective of the world and shape the value system of the beliefs we transmit through our communications, choices, relationships, and aspirations. Yes, our stories are full of the memories, successes, failures, and experiences we leave to those we have encountered with hopes elements of our stories will be told in the lives of future generations.

In my research on the familial influence on career decisions, I came across families whose stories were so dynamic and impressive that I felt compelled to share their legacies. These legacies, known as family career legacies, stem from over 100 years of hard-work, perseverance, and community that have continued throughout generations. The legacies are captured in the stories each of the family members tell about their careers and involvement in the family business. It is through their narratives, you will understand the concept of family career legacy and hopefully embrace some takeaways that will get you closer to establishing your legacy.

The sharing of these legacies will not only be educational, but inspirational. The next story I would like to share is of the Hankerton family. Their legacy boasts on dignity, values, public service, and child engagement, all viable tools necessary in building a family career legacy. The quote at the beginning of this chapter, is demonstrative through this family.

The Hankerton Family: Legacy of Community

The Hankerton family career legacy spans over 100 years in a small, community-oriented town, with strong values and traditional ways of rural, southern United States. Beginning with John, a German immigrant who migrated to the south with a strong sense of community and business acumen, the Hankerton family embodies legacy with each generation succeeding in the family's established career path and value structure. From John's entrepreneurial endeavors that employed many of the local town residents to his son Richards's legendary career in public service in the same town, the family's career legacy was created and is maintained by the second and third generation of community bankers (Figure 2).

The career stories of this family career legacy are told from the perspectives of the second generation: Rick, Richard's only son, who is the Chairman of the Board for Vision Bank and Sam, Richard's only son-in-law, who is the immediate past president and CEO of Vision bank, and the third generation: Trey, Rick's only son, who is the current president of Vision Bank, and Kevin, Sam's son, who is the vice president of Vision Bank, who are both in their mid-30's.

Start of a Legacy

Pleasantville, a small town hours away from three of the state's largest cities, is the setting for this family career legacy. A town of less than 16,000 residents, is described as being historic, tranquil, and unified, where men once used to gather at local cafes to talk about the news, politics, livestock, and farming. At that time, Pleasantville's economy included ranching, cotton farming, and oil production and the entrepreneurial ventures of John Hankerton, owner and founder of a wholesale company and a coffee company that originated a national coffee brand. Regarded as a brilliant man, John spoke four languages which allowed him to communicate with European immigrant farmers and merchants who had settled in the area because of the bountiful farming conditions.

During this time, the environment in Pleasantville was one of pride, hard work, tradition, independence, and religion, where neighbors helped one another and embodied the lands friendly culture. This environment found comradery between families and business as children were expected to assist with their family's livelihood. As such, Richard was no stranger to working at both of his father's businesses. In doing so, the Hankerton's value system, rooted in the town's culture, was manifested by John, a businessman who imparted these values to his son Richard and then Richard to his son Rick.

Rick recalled a story,

Grandfather John Hankerton, started the Pleasantville Wholesale and one of the things that affected Dad (Richard) a great deal, that I think affected me, is Dad was a great football player, he was playing at the university and the Depression hit and Grandfather John had to fire about half the people that he had and let them go. And Dad had to come back and save the business during the Depression. One of the first things he had Dad do was to take a knife and crack some eggs, not to badly, and put some slices in flour sacks, and not real bad either. And Dad thought maybe his father (John) had just lost it (laughs) and said "Dad why am I doing this?" And his father said "Son, now there's one thing you need to understand and I think is very important, that in life there are different things that make people do what they do' and he said 'the great driving force is dignity' a man's dignity". And he said, "You've got to respect that for every man and whatever you do and how you do it and it has to be that philosophy and that approach". And he said "the people that I let go helped me build this business".

He said "I can't keep them with the half that I'm hiring and paying now, I won't be able to afford them either. We'd go under. If I also tried to give them things, half of them wouldn't take it because of that dignity and the other half that did, would lose that dignity. So I owe it to them to try to make it possible to recognize that dignity and help them. If I have damaged goods, I can ask them to help me move some things and give them that, which I do, what I'm obligated to do, and they keep the dignity and we do the things that work". He said "that's why you need to do things and do it well".

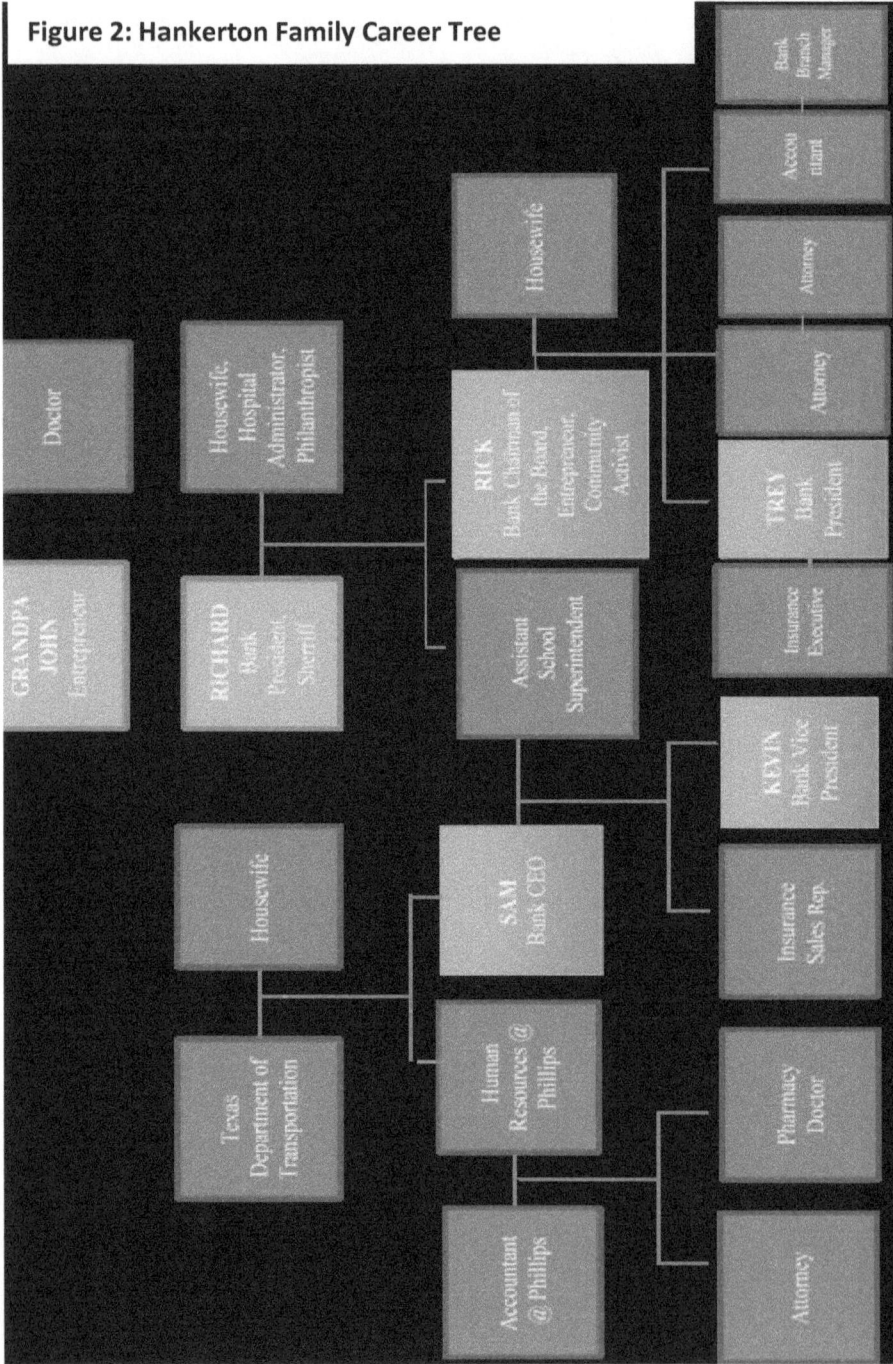

Figure 2: Hankerton Family Career Tree

Beginning of a Career Legacy

This story of business values stuck with Richard even as he transitioned from running his father's coffee company to pursuing his calling in public service, where he ran for sheriff and won. Richard, described by his son as a large man, standing over six feet tall and 240 pounds, with scarred hands from bouts in his law enforcement duties and WWII, was intimidating in presence. Rick compared his dad to the fictional, crime-fighting sheriff John Wayne; stating he looked, walked, and spoke like Wayne, the only difference was Richard carried a long ten-cell flashlight nicknamed "The Light of Enlightment" instead of a gun because he believed that violence was not a resolution. In his job as sheriff, Richard sought to build trust between citizens and law enforcement with non-discriminatory practices, training of youth, and a disregard for mistreatment of others. Richard's courteous but no nonsense demeanor led to him earning the moniker of "The Peacemaker," which is now an award named in his honor given to law enforcement officials that demonstrate his career mantra of "you have to try to bring out the best in man not the worst in him".

After a legendary career as sheriff, Richard made a pivotal career change to become a community banker at Vision Bank with the purpose to provide for the future of his family and the Pleasantville community. Vision Bank, founded in 1933, is a staple in Pleasantville, known for its old-fashioned hospitality, quality service, and heart for the community. Even presently, Vision's mission is "Our people, our service, our best." With three branches in three nearby towns, the legacy of the Hankerton family, started by Richard through his leadership in the late 1950's, 60's and early 70's, still lives on in the memories of his children, grandchildren, great grandchildren, and community.

Richard's career legacy was passed on to his son through what was a generative epilogue of values, reflection, and advice for his son Rick, in the final days of his life. Richard said

The most important thing I can leave you is a good name, and I think I have done that. Your mother and I have worked and saved a long time to create this beginning for you and your sister. Home has always been the most important part of our lives

and should be yours. We hope we have taught you the importance of our values and passed along our heritage. You have an education that will help you achieve what is really important in life--being a responsible citizen, loving husband, and sensitive father...What I feel I will be leaving you is an opportunity—a start from which you can make your own mark....All we can do within our life span is to make the world better than it was when we first arrived...Teach your children the ideals you think are proper. Give them the best values that you can. And teach them how to judge what is best for their lives and nation. We must try to make every generation's character better than the one before it and build a higher standard of living through wise policies. The rule of the world is not just to take from life, but to put something back.

Second Generation

Those final words from his father have affected the life and career decisions of Rick, who has written books around the values his father taught him and expressed before his passing. Rick, a jolly, warm and friendly man, embodies the southern culture with a firm handshake and a southern accent. His office was a suite, with numerous plaques and pictures decorating the beige walls, documenting the various international, national, and local interactions Rick has had with various organizations and people. Beyond this first area was his office, another large space filled with trophies and framed wall certificates acknowledging his many achievements and organizational and community involvements. He had a mahogany wooden desk that sat directly in front of large, bay windows with a mahogany matching wall cabinet to the right and a small round table on the left with two regular office chairs. His office seemed updated from the drab décor in the bank lobby. He offered me seat at the table to conduct the interview where he reflects on the family career legacy and his contribution to further the legacy for the third and fourth generations. Here, Rick narrates his career story.

RICK'S STORY

I think the family area was important because I had a good amount of respect for Dad. For 20 years he was a sheriff in Ford County and it was only about for

12 years he was a banker. But what he liked about banking and emphasized is that it was a really good profession because you could serve the people. And it was a case impart where you risked your own money, you weren't making money off people but with people and that was particularly important to him. He also greatly liked the fact of dignity. The bank may have been a small bank, but he was president of a bank and he had the opportunity to do what he wanted to do. He could be an independent type person. Now it didn't make that much money but it gave you the opportunity to do the things that you felt were important, that were more of what you valued. A lot of the things in our family, I think that he taught me and my mother taught me learned a lot with people.

FAMILY BEGINNINGS

Dad had been in the military, mother had come from a family of doctors and so she was sort of cultured and Dad was sort of reality of hunting and other type things. Mother had a…they were both strong personalities. And they were equally important to what happened to us. Dad was a trained commander of war, very tough man. Dad was one of the gentlest souls, nicest people you'd ever run into but tough as nails. Mother was very cultured, very refined, from a family that much more focused on us being sure we got our schooling, our education… We had two very different influences but very important ones that shaped a lot of what you ended up doing. They spent a lot of time helping me with learning, got me to understand how important an education was. They were sort of opposites that attracted but they had the same values, it gave me a very balanced upbringing. So to a large extent, it was a solid family of values.

Oh grandfather, Grandfather John was a founder of the Pleasantville Wholesale, he was in the book of the, the…Stephen F. Austin the major business man. Uh so he was fairly legendary. My grandfather on my mother's side died at 42. He had gotten exposed to a very lot. He was an extremely well known doctor; there were probably seven Drs. Wilkins, all the doctors. They were a large medical family. He had trained a lot of the people that had the fevers, plus he had got pneumonia during WWI, so a lot of that effect probably got him and he just had a heart attack. But he was, probably his best friend was Dr. Jeff, from Jeff and Jeb, were doctors so he would have been a very prominent doctor had he lived cause he established a lot. So most of the family has had, in one place or another, we have achieved a genealogy that goes back on both sides kind of tracing some of the history because I think it's very important for people to know from whence you come. And it's not just the genetics; it's a lot of the values.

My family, I grew up in a garage apartment. Our families had had money but Grandfather Wilkins died at 42 (laughs) so the Wholesale rested on this, it wasn't like they hadn't great educations but they built everything on you know what they had. And we sacrificed in order to get there. It was sort of my job to keep sacrificing; it takes two to three generations of a family a lot of times to build things.

The things that helped build Pleasantville were a lot of banks took a lot of risks in the beginning to bring in the jobs. The rest, it was two or three times the size of the other cities. Back then that environment of economic growth that you kinda had to do this. The state was moving out of just rural agricultural deal to getting more involved in the world and had to have more of the economic development, so that became very key.

EXISTENCE OF CAREER INFLUENCES AND ROLE MODELS

The main thing is I really enjoyed learning. What Mother and Dad, probably Mother more than Dad, emphasized to me is that you never can quit learning. The more you can understand, the more you can get, the more you can gain and knowledge is what matters. So once Mother sort of taught me that, Dad taught me the realities of life of how you actually have to look at the world and participate in it and not to be afraid of it but to charge forward, cause temperament is very important. Having a focus or an ambition for the future, Mother gave me, having a temperament and a reality perspective, Dad gave me. And the two kind of combined in me that, you know, I love learning. That's why I gotten involved in a lot of different things in that direction since then. Dad was a significant influence, I worked at the bank in the summers. I learned a lot more about how banking worked. Two or three of his friends were fairly major investors that taught me a lot about, got me books about insurance companies, the new gold of the future, and how different things worked. So I got a little different impression of what probably was of interest to me.

FAMILY VALUES

I think Dad emphasized dignity, integrity, honor, and um the particular values of conscience. If you had one area that separated two things, you have, you live your life by conscience and convenience. Dad, when he was sheriff resigned so he could go to WWII. So that value orientation probably more than how much money you made and I mean he did well and we've been successful in what we did. But that isn't what drove why you did what you did, the motivation. They never were that interested in maybe how much money we ended up making but were probably much more interested in what people not so much thought but what we thought of ourselves and how things came about to get it done. The whole bank here is a family, so it's not just our family. So we try to teach everybody here, we try to do what we can do for their different directions. It's what values fit in, goes back to Dad learning from his father. Dignity is what matters and relationships is what matter.

PRESSURE

Compared to Dad, probably, I just want to keep, he made it real clear to me, he was giving to me a very good name and I better keep it straight and I don't want him to roll over in his grave or look at me from above, so I think that's important. With Mother I think the issue is kindness. Mother was one who really, she would make cookies for the prisoners in jail and Christmas. She was just a very kind Christian person and believed in a lot of different type things. So I believe I feel a constant pressure to help start charities. Conscience is obligation and its compassion combined. And those are some things that matter a great deal. So I think there's a lot of pressure in the sense to me, I understood in the concept of my family's generation, shame mattered, you had a sense of a certain obligation you had to do and I don't know if that is prominent any now as it was then but it sure stayed with me. The concept of guilt of doing what you needed to do and why you did it, motivation.

SENSE OF BELONGING AND COMMUNITY

In each case, we've had in our family, speaking we have three kids. My oldest daughter is Shan, she and her husband are both lawyers, they both have business degrees. Trey is here with his wife Sunny and they have three kids. She's an insurance executive, he's at the bank. My daughter Brianna works with the local accounting firm, um her husband runs our other branch. I think the thing we've found is how do you combine and continue to work as a family unit. Um in a lot of cases everything we've ever done has been, more or less, orienting people to have their own choices in what and where they wanted to go. But opportunities, if they wanted to do some of these different things that everybody would try to help them accomplish what they wished.

I think what I said before, it gives a degree of independence. It gave me a sense of dignity that matters, you also got why you do that matters. You make money with people rather than off of people. A lot of professions are selling something that is here. Here if money gets lost, it's our money mostly, capital. It's not somebody else's so... We had a case, that's why I would never want the bank to fail, the rest of the good things, that sense of honor kind of matters. So you have a case that you want to get at least through, so you feel that you have an unfinished thing, you wanna still solidify with everything that's there is important.

I've been spending a lot of time with different groups trying to help build bridges. And I think that if there's a deal in life that I like to kind of finish. We've taken on a financial literacy project that uh is trying very hard to look at how do you educate. If you look at, we can't make a lot of successful loans to younger people because their credit is already ruined by the time they come and rules tell us you need... (laughs) You have one set of rules to protect consumers and you got a case where the kids have been given student loans and everything else before they get there.

So I got five major corporations and a whole bunch of others that we are trying to put on a literacy project, it's called the Dignity Alliance. What we're trying to do is get the right curriculum put together that will let kids understand the importance, they will understand finance and how to do certain things in order to then see what opportunities there are, why education is necessary. In order to then, to keep dignity. And that's something I'd really like to see, we got working on it quite a bit, Trey's helped with it and it's not any organized effort beyond something that really matters. The biggest problem that kids have is maybe the families themselves haven't had the perspective of giving the certain ambition of what you can become. It's not as much ambition; it's an understanding of what you can achieve.

The whole bank here is a family, so it's not just our family. So we try to teach everybody here, we try to do what we can do for their different directions. It's what values fit in, goes back to Dad learning from his father. Dignity is what matters and relationships is what matter.

MAKING MEANING OF CAREER EXPERIENCES

When reminiscing of how he came to follow in the banking footsteps of his father, Rick discussed his dad's influence on his college choice and how his involvement with the bank at a young age helped to secure his career fate.

You know looking at different universities, he [Dad] had read at one place there was a professor who had been a person who had sold cars and was very practical. Dad read a couple of articles and one of these fellas out of Harvard, basically was all theory and the professor was talking about 'here's how the numbers work'.

(laughs) He said, 'I think you ought to go and work for this guy'. (laughs) Dad had gone to the university, so it was a case that I was probably looking at, and they had a great business school and so I decided then that's probably really what I wanted to do.

Because I learned banking, I worked in banking my summers, when I was in high school. Basically, I've worked in the bank sorting checks for my summer deals. It looked to me something that I had kind of enjoyed. I think Dad had looked at me to probably come back but didn't push me to do so and so I had, I thought about probably being a lawyer and he thought it would be good for me to be a lawyer as well. So um, I went to the Navy for the Vietnam era. I was in the thing called the Insul 95 program. There were 120 to 30,000 people, they took 80. Everybody there was pretty much a valedictorian of their class or university. But that program was very unique in shaping me because you had 80 really smart people competing against each other, some from north, south, different directions. The first time I had really been intensely in with a lot of people that thought differently than I did but still were intelligent people. So it taught a lot to me to look at diverse type thoughts and ideas and there aren't just right answers, there's a way of thinking through to get things done. Career wise that Navy experience shaped me a lot.

I went to law school after but uh I enjoyed law but it just wasn't the same. But I didn't enjoy it as much as the independence of the banking. At one point, I had not only a law license and practicing law in the courts, I had a security license, a real estate license, an insurance license and a variety of others. When Dad died, Vietnam was over, they didn't need, they preferred to have line officers rather than jag officers. They were happy about when I went to the Reserves, so I ended up going to the Reserves. I left there a lieutenant commander, I stayed in the Reserves for a long time.

Oh, I think that Dad, it was always perceived that Dad would like for me to come back and run the bank. So I think that was always a little bit in the back of my mind, whether we did that or not, that was not a driving factor because if I could find a better thing somewhere else, or if I was gonna do this. And in part what Dad didn't but Mom didn't want me to do, they felt that Pleasantville might be a little limiting. Because of some of the other records I had had and what other people told them I could probably do and so they didn't push that at all. Um and I really didn't decide to come back and do the banking here until Dad's death and I had to come back up. Well when Dad died, the problem is the other two officers that had been very prominent in the bank had died just right before him, had cancer.

So the question was 'do we sell the bank or do we try to keep it?' And it was a very small bank, about $16 million in size and wasn't making that much money. So it was sort of a family asset, so I took it on. Dad had borrowed money to um buy his stock in it and I took on much of his debt and really from there it was the case, if I was gonna do this or we just sold it, and we wanted to keep it as a family deal and that had been a lot of what Dad really wanted. So that was kind of, with Mother there, the rest of it that kind of made the determination.

From there, I think Claire [my wife] and I just decided this was a great place to raise kids. And the other things I wanted to do were public service more than just monetary type areas because you were limited to a small bank you couldn't do a lot of other things in business. I mean I had the chance to go to Harvard and most other directions, but I really, and when I looked at what I have done, I've had a chance to do a lot of things in life. But basically, what made community banking important is that it's really what Dad originally said, its something you can help other people. You may not do as much as you could in other places but its independence and it's a dignity that gives you something that's there, it's what you value.

The good thing about community banking is it's a little bit different. It lets you do a lot of the things that you like to do and it lets you help people. And at the same time you can do well enough in it that you take care of your family and you also get the right values. I mean everything he taught me based on honor and the importance of dignity, those type of areas. But there also was a very conscience effort to make sure that I got a broadened education and understood how to work with people and work with situations, so it wasn't an overly protected one.

You could be involved in the activities, I was president of the local chamber of commerce and state chairman, just as Dad. And Dad was very involved in public politics, civic activities, and economic development. So the good thing, being the banker, was kind of opportunity for a broad-based area, where a lot people are very sector focused from the bottom up. The banking opportunity gave one from the top down with a broader range of things that guided you. Then you get a very different perspective, it isn't that you have a job, per say, it's not that you have an occupation, it's that you have a calling. And the calling is a significant part, a lot to it beyond what you just do.

There's not one profession, it's a sense of judgment that you get and the judgment comes from experiences in a lot of places. And so, you kind of say in the end, what is it that is our family's job. Is it banking? I don't think it's really banking, I think its involvement. And it's really a broader concept of what you want to do in life. Banking makes a lot of the rest of it possible. But the rest of what is possible that we do is part of the core of banking because it's our reputation, what do we do, how do we do it, how do things work?

I sit on the board of Blue Cross Blue Shield and (inaudible) out of Illinois the biggest nonprofit insurance company and what we study is culture. And the culture within the corporation and it matters a huge degree how that culture dictates from the top, how people understand it and how people see it and what they do with it and how it fits together. And Corporate America is beginning to see the absolute importance of that and it's not just compliance of keeping people upright. It's the conscience of them being upright. And there is a huge difference in style of what's taught, how it's taught, how it's transmitted, this is one of the cutting edge deals moving forward. You take Blue Cross, I'm chair of their finance committee with a highest rated insurance company in our field by everybody, so and we're a nonprofit, so it's not that we don't understand how to operate. The question is, what values do we have and how do we operate?

And I think Mom and Dad would have been the happiest with that because when you look back and it says 'how did you live your life, or what did you do?' They never were that interested in maybe how much money we ended up making but were probably much more interested in what people not so much thought but what we thought of ourselves and how things came about to get it done.

I was always one that believed you needed to save the world. Just like Dad believed you needed to have responsibilities. You teach your kids, you belong to civic deals, we've all been Chamber heads, you know, this, that or the other. So a lot of what also affected us, what I go about banking isn't a profession, it's a part of the profession of involvement. A good part of the other deal is we made all the loans here for the industrial foundation. The things that helped build Pleasantville were a lot of banks took a lot of risks in the beginning to bring in the jobs. The rest, it was two or three times the size of the other cities. Back then that environment of economic growth that you kinda had to do this. The state was moving out of just rural agricultural deal to getting more involved in the world and had to have more of the economic development so that became very key.

But basically, what made community banking important is that it's really what Dad originally said, it's something you can help other people. You may not do as much as you could in other places but its independence and it's a dignity that gives you something that's there, it's what you value. I've had partnerships in New

York with investment banking; I've had opportunities for partnerships in Mexico. These books get written by the major, the supporting group in China that trains all their leadership. So I've seen much of the rest of the world. And Dad was pretty much correct. The dignity and the ability of what you value matter. It's whether you care about other people and the future or whether you care about yourself and now. An awful lot of professions, an awful lot of things ended up in that convenience deal on how do I make money or how can I get in politics with the ambition.

The good thing about community banking is it's a little bit different. It lets you do a lot of the things that you like to do and it lets you help people. And at the same time you can do well enough in it that you took care of your family and you also get the right values. And that's probably where I would sit in and that's where my kids, I hope Trey's son ends up going in the same direction too.

You had a lot of generations in politics, civic service and the rest of it. I mean each of 'em if you take this generation did this, my generation about the same thing, Trey's already done the types of things, and RJ will sort of grow up understanding each of the different areas of what sort of was past him.

CONTINUING THE LEGACY

In my family, I probably do most of the...for when we were growing up, we put savings in each of the kids' names. At 18 they had it for their education, they could spend it, do it, what they want to do, however they want to do it. A lot of people do trust or other type of directions, we don't. Our family was much more oriented to teaching them responsibility, in a lot of the different areas and said look 'we're gonna help you with the rest of it, we'll do that, but this is more than enough to get you through college but if you don't spend all of it and you handle it well, you'll have enough to probably buy a house or do something else with it as well'. I think it taught responsibility to each of the kids before they ever got there.

I set most of the things up because I have the background to do that. Each of the kids run their families independently. I help them and we look at joint things as a family, you know, what may be a benefit long term, how does this work? I mean, we have things, that's the equivalent a little bit of sort of working like a family office in a company called Hankerton Venture Capital Corporation, where they own parts. We do types of investments but generally everybody sort of does their own. All of the kids have at least masters or law degrees. They've all got business degrees, I mean husbands and spouses both, so they're very different than us. So it's a very educated family to that extent.

34

One of the things that was beneficial to us was my father was a very influential man. We had begun to learn, I made sure my kids knew, everything and when he died, I was younger, a lot of these friendships weren't in place yet, they got into place more of the years I was here cause I would find, they would say 'I knew your dad, I was your dad's friend' this that or the other, so getting a perspective of the world broader than Pleasantville was critically important. And I think for families having a perspective of what the future's gonna be.

I make sure that every one of our kids, there are five newsletters that I buy for each of them: I buy the Economist for each of them, I buy the Financial Times, they see a lot broader deal. Now they may not read it but I think it's critically important that that perspective be there. And the way you think about things. The key in life is how you think about something determines what you think about it. Critical point, so shaping that perspective about how do you think, is absolutely essential. That's really what these books, there's a set of triangles on the back of them that talk about here's how you go through taking basically the powers and the functions. Basically the forces, the forces are changed based on the status quo, which is really the power of history moving forward in the culture. And how those two interact and that's the basis of what you talk about here.

The main thing we found a long time ago is Dad sort of told me that I could, he would support me in any way you wanted to and he'd help me in any direction, we'd do some things together but basically there's a, every unit is sort of built independently where they do what they have and in some cases we come together to do things as a unit. In other words, I'd have a family corporation that we have oil and gas interests and other types of things in that we may do certain deals out of them where everybody has a part, sort of like a family office but each of them runs their own individual family areas, each of the education, where people help with kids, grandkids, where they take on things.

Its better when they have the independence and responsibility so that they think in terms of responsibility and then you build the other, older generation as a support network of looking to see how it comes together. A lot of people will build family partnerships. I'm not in, for our family, a family partnership didn't necessarily work that well because usually with a family partnership you take assets then sort of distribute them out. We built a corporation that was a sub-s called Hankerton Venture Capital Corporation, all of them are officers of it and directors. To a great extent, everything that's sort of done in that entity they get there, they learn, just like the bank where they're involved with it. You got different committees and structures that people see, learn to make the decisions.

I think they give me new respect since the fact I spent a lot of time putting this together over the years, took all the debts for the rest to get there but to a great extent they do their things. And they're the next bullets in the game. There's a good friend of mine who is a Congressman, Chair of the Economic Committee, you know when he was giving some of the speeches of these awards, either he or one of the people with him said you know 'the Hankertons usually reload' in other words it's the next generation (laughs).

You had a lot of generations in politics, civic service and the rest of it. I mean each of 'em if you take this generation did this, my generation about the same thing, Trey's already done the types of things, and RJ will sort of grow up understanding each of the different areas of what sort of was past him and so the books are as much for them to learn. I don't think many other people are going to be interested in reading a lot of, I was surprised that the reaction to them, a lot of them were written for family because it's the only way you can put forth the ideas and thoughts that you actually got.

Because it always says to shirt sleeves to shirt sleeves and three generations you basically have a case of, and the same thing they say in China, you'll have one generation that works hard, one generation that learns from it, the next one loses it. And so we're real conscience of that so we were (laughs with me) very focused that what comes in and how it goes generationally. So I think a lot of what we had has been a family education of how to get it down.

I think you leave an honorable reputation, ah you've haven't cheated anybody or done anything. I think in my life I've accomplished most of the different things that in that sense that I think are important. What I would like to do is get two or three things, you ask what is unfinished? A few of the last things I want to do with the family corporation is get it set and I'm getting that done. You know the bank, the same way, I want to sort of turn it over a little bit to Trey and the next generation.

SAM'S STORY

The second component to the second generation is Sam, the son-in-law to Richard, brother-in-law to Rick, and father to Kevin. Sam, with southern charm, greeted me with a firm handshake and invited me to sit at the round table in his office. He wore khaki pants and a polo shirt, which was business casual compared to the business professional attire of Rick. At the table, he asked me about my progress in the doctoral program and about my career plans after graduation. After our brief conversation, he gives his account of his family background and how his career story is part of the Hankerton family career legacy.

Kevin's grandfather, Mr. Hankerton, who was the first banker in this family, was larger than life. A sheriff for 25 or 30 years here in Ford County, retired into the banking business. Both of those jobs are people jobs and he was, as I said, a larger than life person. He was physically imposing, he had a very important job being county sheriff and retired from that into being a bank president. So that's a lot to live up to. It certainly qualifies as a legacy that would be difficult to live with for some folks.

FAMILY BEGINNINGS

We [me and my brother] grew up in a very small community outside Windham, and my dad was so respected within the community that I could remember people coming by in the evenings to visit with my dad about problems they might be having. He helped people do their income tax returns, he provided advice and counseling to them, without even knowing that's what he was doing.

My dad worked for the state highway department for his entire career. He worked 41 years and retired with the highway department, so he was, uh, he's one of the smarter guys I've ever known but he didn't have a college degree. He could have but in those days with the war effort and everything else that was going on in his life, fighting and coming out of the Depression, etc., he didn't have the opportunity to go to school.

EXISTENCE OF CAREER INFLUENCES AND ROLE MODELS

And the, the career I ended up being involved with, being a community banker, is so much more, in my opinion, community than it is banker. Uh and I think my dad instilled that desire to be a part of a small community within me without even knowing he was trying to do that. My wife was probably the most important person that encouraged me to go ahead and do something different, if that's what I wanted to do.

That is so hard to answer but I guess I'll say my dad cause, as I said earlier, he was an extremely intelligent guy. He's one of those guys that could do anything. Grew up on a farm and he could repair anything, he could build on to the house, he could fix the tractor, whatever had to be done he could do it. So he combined both professionalism in his career as well as family; he was an unbelievable family man, and a role model for me, uh very religious, a man of great faith.

So I'd have to say that I admired that probably the most; however, having said that, my mom was a stay-at-home all her life. But she was always, always there. I was a high school athlete. I went to a small high school, so you did everything athletic, every sport. I don't ever remember a game that one or both of my parents were not present. So what I'm saying is they both provided such support that it's a hard question to answer when you ask me 'who I admired the most'. They're both right there on that pedestal. Having said that, I'd have to say my dad, if I had to make a choice.

PRESSURE

I had one sibling, an older brother. He also has an MBA and was very successful with Phillips Oil in his career. He too was an HR person in his career with Phillips. His wife also worked with Phillips, she got her undergraduate degree in accounting. My brother's son is an attorney; his daughter is a doctor of pharmacy. My wife, as I said, has her doctorate. My brother-in-law is an attorney. All three of his children have their MBAs. Both of my sons have their MBAs. What I'm saying is I'm as little educated as anybody in the family. So sometimes I can look out and say, 'you know, I'm the dumbest kid on the block'.

I'm just trying to show though that there is a certain amount of pressure when the entire family reunion is as educated or more so than you are. So it it's an interesting question for me to try to answer. I do feel that pressure and I do feel that I guess probably looking back on myself, a little self-psychology here, that I probably look at myself as the underachiever.

And looking back I think they [my sons] felt a pressure all along to at least acquire a post undergraduate degree of some kind, which leads to that economic pressure or position that you are referring to. As I told you earlier, my wife has her doctorate of education. I have a MBA, so it was just naturally understood in our household growing up that they certainly would acquire at least an undergraduate degree and hopefully, preferably some kind of post-graduate degree. So I think they felt some kind of pressure to do that.

38

Community banking itself is under such great pressure both from a regulatory perspective and from an economic perspective with the rate cycle being where it is now and has been there so long. We have no idea when that economic pressure is going to ease up, if it indeed ever does. Uh, so I told Kevin when he decided to come back and work for us here at Vision Bank that there are no guarantees because I could see a possibility that community banking itself could meet its demise. However, there are no guarantees anywhere in life. He had a desire to come back here for what reason, I'm not sure, I hope he shared that with you. Uh, but I didn't want him to feel that there was pressure for him to come back to Vision Bank but I do fear that there's not going to be the same opportunities for him or his generation to be as successful in this business as we have been in the past. So I do, I feel that pressure and I do feel there could be some unfinished business there that may or may not be achievable not because that generation is failing to achieve but because the opportunity may not be there due to outside influences.

SUPPORT
Uh, as a family, on both sides of my family, my parents and siblings, and my wife and her side of the family both are very tight knit family units. So uh, they [my parents] certainly supported education, helped me through, all the way through my undergraduate degree but did not really, what I would say provide me with any particular direction in which to go. Also, my wife, she was the biggest motivator in my career. We've had now a 44 year marriage, so we kinda rely on one another and so she was highly and has always encouraged me in other things as well. Uh, nothing specific comes to mind when I think of emotional, a sense of stories or concern but they were both and we were both very close to our families growing up and even until our parents died. So they were very supportive of what we did both emotionally and in any other way.

FAMILY VALUES
The dominant family values from both sides, the golden rule: treat others as you would wished to be treated. Respect others no matter who and what they are. Uh I don't know if I've ever said it to them in those words, but I can remember saying to both boys when they were small, do the right thing for the right reason and everything else will take care of itself. So that's the only rule I can come up with having actually stated to those kids.

MAKING MEANING OF CAREER EXPERIENCES

My very first job as a child was probably when I was 15 or 16 years old. Well, let me go back even before that, I don't call this a real job but growing up on a small farm, we had a cub tractor with a mower on it. I would mow lawns and small pastures for the neighbors, so Dad let me use the tractor during the day when he was at work; it had to be there when he got home though because he needed it to do stuff around the farm. So that's the first thing I remember to make a little money that I did.

My first full-time job after getting married was teaching school for one year and then I was drafted and served in the army for two years. I guess my earliest career ambition would be going back to when I was in the army. I did not serve in Vietnam but through the luck of the draw only, I was expected to receive orders to go to Vietnam but my orders came down and I spent my entire military career stateside.

Uh I taught school for a year or so before I got drafted and uh my wife and I were actually talking one day about what we were going to do when we got out of the army because I didn't want to go back to teaching school. So I decided at that point and time, she was also teaching school but she wanted a career in education, so she wanted to go back and get her masters and hopefully at that time her doctorate, which she eventually did. But I didn't want to go back to teaching school so I decided I wanted to go back to graduate school but get an MBA instead of an advancing degree in education.

During that army time, my father-in-law who was president of this bank at the time, passed away. So uh at that point and time I didn't know what I was going to do with that MBA but I decided that's what I wanted to do. Then the opportunity came up, but I guess what motivated me to get into business was just the fact that I decided teaching was not my calling.

Rick, my brother-in-law, came back to run the bank, he was in the Navy at the time, he received a hardship discharge to get out of the Navy and come back and take the job as president of the bank. And then as I was working on my MBA, he's the one that recruited me to come here to work. So as they say, the rest is history. That was in 1975 that I came here, so I've been here at Vision Bank since 1975.

I started as a teller. Worked as a teller for a short-time then started doing various, what I call, odd job management chores. The first thing I tried to do, was we had an older gentlemen that worked at the time more or less as our PR person. He knew everybody in the county. He had worked selling tractors for his whole career and he was probably between 75 and 80 years old at the time and he just went to work for the bank trying to be our PR guy. He'd take me out in the afternoons and introduce me to everybody he knew in the county. So that was the first thing I tried to do was to learn our customer base. Uh, (pause) I guess I was here two to four years before I started into the lending side of the bank and from there worked up into this position.

My career decisions seemed to evolve rather than be sought out. In fact my career choice didn't occur till I was married and had gotten that post-graduate degree. My parents didn't influence my career choice. But what appeals to me the most about my career choice is people! Simple but true.

CONTINUING THE LEGACY

I hope to leave a sense of pride. I hope they could look back on my career, my wife's career, Rick's career and say that we did something for the bank, for the family, and probably more importantly for the community that they can look at and be proud of and what more can a man do. My meaning of success: being happy at what you do while helping others achieve and achieving some level of success yourself.

Third Generation

The third generation interview of the Hankerton family includes Trey, Rick's son, who is the current bank president and Kevin, Sam's son, who is the vice president. These two young men were groomed to take leadership of the bank and after meeting these pleasant and very southern men, they share their career stories with me in their individual offices.

Trey's office was located on the first floor down a hallway away from the lobby. A regular-sized square office, Trey had a large Navy banner on the wall behind his desk, as well as other Navy paraphernalia on the walls. There were a lot of boxes behind his desk and two regular office chairs that sat in the front of his desk. He had a few pictures of his wife and kids in frames on top of other items in his office. He stood about 5'8 and was conservatively dressed with gray pants and a blue collared, button-down dress shirt. He appeared to be a younger version of his father.

Kevin's office was on the second floor, near his father's current office. His office was bare at the time of the interview, given he only had been there two weeks. However, it was a large space with windows with a view. Like his father's office and Rick's, he had a small round table near the door and a wooden desk with two large office chairs. Kevin, in contrast to his cousin Trey, was about 5'11 and had a thin-build. Like his cousin, his appearance was neat with the same type of attire and the common southern accent.

Trey and Kevin, both new to their positions at the time of their interviews, acknowledged their position as third generation bankers and expressed respect and gratitude to the previous generations for their foundation. Trey and Kevin both share a story about their grandfather Richard. Trey begins,

Well on the legends piece, I think the biggest thing I've learned through customers is the stories about my grandfather. Um there was a customer, that ended up being a customer of mine, but was a customer of my grandfather's and he would come in and say that my grandfather would, he had an office right there on the lobby floor in the main bank there when it was downtown. Uh and he would be there and when he saw him walk in the door he would come and shake his hand and come and talk to him. Um there's also a story about um my grandfather being asked by an examiner the security policy and he pointed to the shot gun (both he and author laugh) in his office and he said, um basically the examiner said 'you got to have something written down' and so that night he wrote something up and uh one of the cashiers, Johnny Miller, came in the bank and saw him typing. First thing in the morning he was typing it up and he went through a long, basically the story was, the policy was that basically anytime a robber would be or come into the bank, he'd be corralled and put into a man-hole (he and author laugh). My grandfather had a security experience so there were always stories like that about my grandfather. You know he seemed to be a larger than life character.

Kevin gives a similar sentiment account of his grandfather Richard. He stated

My grandfather worked at this bank. He unfortunately passed away about 20 years before I was born, so I didn't get to know him but he was a volunteer sheriff that became, he got elected as sheriff, excuse me, he got elected as sheriff here so he understood the community, he represented the community, people respected him and for people to come to me today and tell me what they thought of my grandfather that I never got to meet and how of an outstanding individual he was, it, obviously sends chills up your spine when you haven't gotten to meet him but you hear all these wonderful stories. People aren't wonderful if you aren't hearing about them 20 years, 30 years, 40 years after they're deceased. So it started with him, he started working at this bank, he in a way passed it down to his kids, got them involved in a bank, with stock and with other opportunities so that's one generation passing it down to my parents is a second.

FAMILY BEGINNINGS

Trey stated,

Growing up I always wanted to be a banker. Oh I think just early childhood, you know, pre-school. I saw my dad being a banker and something I always wanted to do. I was closest to him, number one and I saw him when he had to…I think my respect grew for him over time but when he came back to the bank he was 25 years old. My grandfather had just died and um there was a need for leadership within the bank and at 25 years old, he provided that. And was able to keep the bank independent and get through some difficult times, I think that just watching him go through that was admirable.

On the other hand, Kevin talks about his perspective of his family beginnings and the role of his mother and father.

Oh it's really a long story from the very beginning of my education process at the point where I was able to understand what education was all about. High school and beyond, my parents had always enforced education. My mom was a doctoral student herself, graduated with a doctorate in education. So she's been the assistant superintendent at Pleasantville Independent School District for over 35 years, recently retired. So she's always known the value of education. My father himself has an MBA, so he knew that education was the key to success, really, in what you wanted to do. So from a very early age, it wasn't, my family was based around education, it wasn't 'where are you going to go to college', it was 'when you graduate college what are you going to do afterward?' Well growing up in this family, we've, ah, my dad's been in banking himself for over 35 years and so growing up around that kind of made me interested in the idea of banking, what it entails, and then part of it was luck.

But in my family, my father and my mother both retained the same job, looking back they retained the same job my entire life. They've never moved and that consistency helped me develop who I am, so to me it's a whole nother level of a role model. I was raised in a tight knit family. They told me I could do whatever I

43

wanted to do and it just so happened that growing up around it, it ended up being what I wanted to do.

Obviously your dad growing up is always your hero. My father is an avid golfer, so he had my brother and I at the age of three and four out there on the golf course with him. So he's instilled in us the idea of our hobby is golf. And it really is funny you bring that up, cause you learn a lot about a person. You learn a lot about a person and their character and values on the golf course. I'm happy that my parents' generation instilled in me good moral character. That I think, I think golf helped me to build what I am today.

EXISTENCE OF CAREER INFLUENCES AND ROLE MODELS

Here Trey recounted his thoughts on role models, family values, pressure, and support.

I guess to learn from my dad and essentially um make choices based on what I guess other role models in the banking industry have made. Also, regarding external influences, I think just in general [9/11] was a world event that affected me through serving in the Navy reserve for the eight year commitment. I don't know if that was tied to career choice. It was a world event that was happening, kind of all-encompassing at the time.

FAMILY VALUES

(Trey)

I think there's just a sense that we treat each other with respect cause there's always sacrifice when coming back to the bank. You know, where we come from, there's different jobs there in the big city and you're getting paid more money. So there's kind of a respect that when those that have come back to help the family business that we treat each other with respect and that's the main rule. Hard work, education, um I think with all of us there is a sense of ethics, a sense of morality. Um you know and I think that beyond just treating ourselves with respect, we treat others, our employees, shareholders, and customers with respect.

PRESSURE

(Trey)

Well yeah a little bit. Uh not strong but it was always something you know, that I think my dad, towards the end of my grandfather's career he was a banker. So I think my dad saw that um and came back to the bank and helped it grow. And he probably wanted to make sure that it continued and though that we'd be an asset and a vehicle to make that happen. So there was never a sense that you need to come back. I was never forced to come back. But, definitely I think there was a um, from day one he thought that this would be a good business, a good opportunity to help our shareholders if we had you know family members in the bank that also had ownership in the company. I think the biggest pressure is to you know successfully guide the bank into being a successful entity. So I think we all had individual pressures to meet certain milestones.

I think certainly with Dad and Sam there is; I don't feel as much pressure as I do with respect for what they were able to get through. When you talk about the banking industry in the '80's it was a difficult time. They were the only bank in Pleseantville that survived through the financial crisis. Uh I think that whether its pressure or an amount of respect but also an amount of ... kind of making sure we understand how they made the decisions they needed to get through. And if we hit a financial storm, we're able to learn from what they did and be able to survive as well.

But I think both individually and collectively we feel pressure to be, you know, good custodians of the bank. I think ultimately, the way my dad's described it before I think accurately is that ultimately the bank stock is the stock for your grandchildren. You know ultimately you're here to preserve the bank and help the bank grow and also make sure that it's here for the next generation for not only our family but for the entire shareholder base. So I think that's the pressure in and of itself to make sure the bank grows and prospers and is preserved.

(Kevin)

They tried to enforce a masters and some sort, and so it was then, 'when you graduate, where are you going to go to your next step of education and schooling?' So they were setting the foundation and building blocks for myself to succeed. The only thing my parents forced upon me was education and obviously looking back I'm thankful that they did. The only pressures were the ones that I put upon myself. There was no pressure to be a banker.

SUPPORT

(Trey)

My dad encouraged me, um (long pause) you know a family friend, who's been a friend of my dad's and also been an accountant in the industry also encouraged

45

me when I came back to the bank. Uh so he would be another one and other members of my family. My sister encouraged me. So I can't say that anyone discourage me. Certainly my dad, my uncle, my aunt they were all helpful in that process and guiding me and helping me to stay on course. You know their support was mainly hands-off. There are times that are hands on. (laughs)

A great deal of emotional support; I think that my dad was helpful when I made the transition home, so was my Uncle Sam. Uh they were both helpful and my aunt, she as well. You know, I think the biggest, the biggest part is when you go from a career outside the family business and then go to the family business, there is a transition there. I mean it's just not, it's as much as anything um kind of (long pause) I don't know how to put that in words exactly. Certainly, I think before I came back I think everyone was interested in making sure, from a standpoint that I was happy and doing the right things to be successful. Once you come back obviously, I think you do what's right for the bank. You do what's right for our business.

Kevin recalled the existence of career influences and role models in his career decision making.

Well again, back to my family, it means a lot, my entire family. A lot of people, I would say a lot of people don't use their family just because they have the personal relationship with them. Both my parents, their education backgrounds were extremely strong. My uncle [Rick], had an extremely strong background, he graduated from the business school. He was the first student to graduate with a 4.0. He then pursued, he has a law degree as well on top of that. He's actually the chairman of this bank. So he's the one that has the vision and the ability to see and interpret the laws and the regulations and see where we're going. He's the strategic planner here. Does a fantastic job and that's why this bank is so fantastic. Those three individuals right there, really set building blocks for my future at such a young age.

MAKING MEANING OF CAREER EXPERIENCES

Trey stated,

I saw my dad being a banker and something I always wanted to do. I worked in bookkeeping here in the bank in the operations department, off and on in the summers. But like I said it changed at some point but it did come full circle. I think that through college that probably changed a little bit. I went to school in '94, graduated in '98 and at that time there were a lot of dot coms forming so I took a job right out of college in information technology. I went to an IT based company in a major city, worked there for two years and was a contractor for larger companies such as Compaq and Waste Management and other local based corporations. So I was mainly IT focused. Then went to grad school and I remember I was working at the local Chamber of Commerce. I graduated from college, got an MBA with a concentration in finance and e-commerce. And [was] finding a way to get experience and then finding a way to come back and be a contributing member to the bank. You know, I think after, probably in grad school I realized there was value in this business, the family business in helping preserve the bank. I guess at that time, I made the decision that banking would be the career for me. And that ultimately went into the bank consulting job out of college cause I wanted to have some experience outside of the bank. Just so that I could help contribute and make the bank stronger when I came back.

And then went to work for a bank consulting company. It's about a 100 employee company and they've got banks across the country. So for two years basically went to different banks and essentially, we had different roles in each bank and I learned a lot about the banking industry and how those banks, you know the consultants they were there, and um basically learned how they went about and analyzed banks. Their methodology for income producing, high income producing banks and how they form banks and banks that were struggling how they helped turn them around. Was able to watch them initially and once I got my bearings on the job and helped to contribute to their turn around. And also I had interaction with clients so I learned a lot about banks, in general.

My dad had encouraged me to find a way to know how banking systems work. He said that was something he didn't have the chance to do when he was 25, he was coming straight from the Navy back to the bank so he didn't have a chance to learn how banks work or how banks' core processing systems work, things like that are kind of the infrastructure of banks. So I wanted to gain that knowledge and then after a couple of years of that I felt like I had a strong knowledge base and I was also getting married and it was kind of a good time to get off the road so that helped contribute to the timing of it. But I think that I made the decision in grad school and took my first job out of grad school with the bank consulting company cause it was an opportunity there and looked to be a good way to gain that banking knowledge. I wouldn't have left there until I felt I had the basic knowledge I needed to come back to the bank but somewhere in that time I gained that and then it was essentially time to come back and help.

Came back here to the bank about 10 years ago and started out in finance. Started out learning under our CFO uh the financial end of the industry and also the operations end of the business, which I had some experience. And then there was an opening here in the retail part of the bank and learned accounting and customer side of the business. Been in this role for about nine years, so the first year was the finance and operations and then last nine have been more customer centered roles. And I guess two years ago was promoted to executive vice-president, then a year or I guess four months ago, promoted to president.

I guess I've been blessed to have a, you now, ah I guess I've always had the freedom to make the choice to come back to the bank. I've always had the freedom to determine. I shouldn't say that exactly, I guess I've always had an opportunity to, I guess to learn from my dad and essentially make choices based on what I guess other role models in the banking industry have made. You know a lot of other bankers started out in the field, you know uh in some way increasing their banking knowledge. Whether that's through being an accountant or you know working in loan review, working for an examination firm or working for one of the examiners. I think that through that, I've been able to have control over the decision I made to get the banking knowledge I need to come back and contribute to the bank.

Things that appeal most to me is helping people in general. I think when you're in banking in particular on the customer side, you get a lot of interaction with people and you can get the opportunity and regulation banking order of essentially to make or give us less and less discretion but there are times when we can help people with whether it's helping their businesses grow, or helping them through a rough patch, helping them get their first car, first home uh those things. Those are the moments that you relish the most. When you're able to help people that you know are doing the right thing to accomplish a goal and you help them get there.

With similar beliefs, Kevin made meaning of his career experiences. *I want to say the first thing I wanted to be was an astronaut but that obviously didn't happen. I don't think…looking back I'm glad it didn't. I'm not really the risk taker here so that worked out really good. You know I really didn't know what I wanted to do. The very first job I ever had, I was a counselor at a little kid's camp. You know when I was 15 years old. I was in a Ford County leadership class when I was in high school but I don't want to say that those were really career building activities because they were so long ago. So I really don't count that as anything building towards my future.*

Pursuing Legacy

My real set of jobs, or my real jobs started I would say at this bank about 11 years ago, I was a part-time teller right out of high school. I went to a junior college for one year, so I was working part-time through that. So I went on, I went to the same university as my grandfather Richard and uncle Rick, did not work while I was there, from there I went to another university immediately after I graduated and got an MBA. So that then led me to the idea, that now that I've gotten the education, the tools, what type of career do I want to do? I was getting out of school, didn't have a job right away, I was a part-time teller at a bank, so I decided, 'whelp, now it's time to really choose a career'.

I had heard ideas about being a bank examiner. You know, I had family, like I've been saying that's been in banking but I didn't know if I wanted to do that. I really did not know what I wanted. Then finally it came to the point where I needed to get a job. I was graduating, I was getting married and I needed a job in the same month. So I decided "well I'm gonna go to this career fair". I had heard about examiners, I was speaking to my family and they kinda told me what they were about and what they were looking for.

I didn't know what I wanted to do until I took my first career job as a banking examiner. They were looking for people at the Department of Banking, that's my first career. And so I then went immediately to the Department of Banking and started falling in love with the idea of banking and what it entailed. National banks have different examiners than state banks. I was state bank examiner so I didn't come to this area to examine this bank but I was able to understand, you know if I took this job I would begin to understand the idea of banking and what it entailed, what went about it, the regulations that governed it, and I guess as soon as I really took that job is where I started to understand.

The next came the Edison Bank job, they, we went and examined Morgan Bank and they came to me a few weeks after and offered me a position. That kind of reinforced the idea "I guess I kind of know what I'm doing, let's give this a shot". That further influenced my decision to stay in banking, I really enjoyed the people I was working with, your mom was one of them. I enjoyed the job, the activities that I was doing, what I was there to do was rewarding; I got to see my work. There's a lot of things that really went into it. And that career, really gave me another set of building blocks to really understand everything about banking from the other side. You know you have the examiners and you have the bankers, and they're two totally different sides. So I was able to understand that side and then came over to the banking side.

That then leaped frogged me into this position. This position became available; the bank thought about me, they wanted to bring me back. My wife and I wanted to come back. And so now that I'm here, I'm happy where I'm at, I think it's a perfect position. I want to be in banking, like I said earlier; I want to continue the legacy of our family I want to continue the legacy of myself. I want to build something of myself; I think this is a wonderful opportunity to do that.

PIVOTAL AND TURNING POINT EXPERIENCES IN CAREER

The two share similar career milestones and life happenings which affected their decision to come and work for the family bank on a full-time basis.

(Trey)

There are a lot of hurdles when you come back. As far as earning respect within the bank and in the business. There are a lot of different things that you have to prove yourself, essentially, to be not only, you know, a member of the family but also a member, a contributing member of the bank to gain people's respect. You know, I think the biggest, the biggest part is when you go from a career outside the family business and then go to the family business, there is a transition there. Probably in grad school I realized there was value in this business the family business in helping preserve the bank. I guess at that time I made the decision that banking would be the career for me. I was also getting married and it was kind of a good time to get off the road so that helped contribute to the timing of it. Well 9/11 was a, it was in grad school so that was around the time. I had already kinda made the decision in my mind that I wanted to come back to the bank and that was definitely an event in the world that was kinda transcendent. I graduated from college and finding a way to get experience and then finding a way to come back and be a contributing member to the bank.

(Kevin)

I was getting out of school, didn't have a job right away, I was a part-time teller at a bank, so I decided, 'whelp, now it's time to really choose a career'. I was graduating, I was getting married and I needed a job in the same month. I didn't know until I was working my first job as an examiner and [Vision] asked me to come back but now that everything is laid out, the cards are laid out, I'm glad that everything happened the way that it did.

SENSE OF BELONGING AND COMMUNITY
A strong sense of belonging to a greater cause through the family career legacy and a quest to be active in the community was noticeable in both Trey and Kevin's stories.

(Trey)

I think right now that the bank has a great reputation in the community, we want to preserve that. I think that the unfinished business is essentially growing the bank. Pleasantville is a growing area, want to make sure we continue to serve Pleasantville and to make sure that we diversify the bank in a way to weather any storm that may hit. There are times when we can help people, whether it's helping their businesses grow, or helping them through a rough patch, helping them get their first car, first home uh those things. Those are the moments that you relish the most. When you're able to help people that you know are doing the right thing to accomplish a goal and you help them get there.

The family is the key to a tremendous amount of a lot of these different things as far as what actually gets imparted and what values people have. I think it becomes important that family matters. Honor matters, all of those different types of things because in the end, that's all you got.

(Kevin)

I came out of the big city, I was there for five years, you get lost in the shuffle, your day consists of waking up, sitting in traffic, going to work, sitting in traffic, coming home. In a small community you don't have all the three hours of traffic that you're sitting in. You have time to get involved; you have time to do things. I wanna be known as someone who gave back to the community he was born in. There is a whole lot more to life in a small town than just going to work and coming home.

You have Chambers of Commerce events where you get out and meet the community. You have all kinds of local businesses that without the support of their local, the people that live in the community, they would fail. So you have all kinds of different avenues that you don't have in the big city. Well if a business fails in larger cities, then it's no big deal. If that business fails here, that could be your brother or one of your best friends from high school that failed, so you have a lot more laying on your shoulders than you did in a larger city. I keep using that as an example because it really does mean a lot to me, to come back here and give back to this community. That's what I want to be known for is someone that gave back, someone that didn't just go to work 9 to 5 and go home. I want to be remembered by anyone that can understand what I was trying to strive to succeed, that I was striving for. The primary role that I want to be known for is gonna be anything that has a positive impact on the community.

It's a give and take here, we thrive off the local community and the local community comes to us when they need a loan. Well if they go to another bank, that hurts us, so it's that give and take relationship with the community that's really strong, so in terms of the bank, I want to see the bank off the charts in success. If it's outside of that, it's the community; I wanna touch back on that. I wanna be involved in the community; I want the community to know that I did what I could for it. I don't expect them to, or honor me in any way, I just want to be able to give back because my mother was raised here, my wife's the fifth generation that's gotten married in this county. We have a lot of lineage here and a lot of family, that's what we want to be known for, is giving back to the community.

CONTINUANCE OF THE LEGACY

The Hankerton family career legacy lives on through the third generation who are poised to succeed their fathers. Their strong sense of belonging is carried over into their thoughts and plans as the next generation of community bankers.

(Trey)

I think by enlarge we want to, and when I say we, I mean Kevin and I and my brother-in-law, I think we want to be good custodians. I think we want to help the bank grow and prosper but you know grow in a way that's prudent and make sure that we make sound financial decisions, sound business decisions, and we want to leave a bank that has the reputation that it has today of being that full-service community bank that's community oriented, that wants to help its customers. We want to continue that tradition and be in a position to continue to grow, you know for the next generation.

I think that success is being able to, you know, by in large being able to be happy where you are in life and to realize that you've done everything you can to help make sure I've got a good name to pass on to my kids uh, that my kids have the start that they need to be successful in life and to be able to have the things they want in life and to be able to make a difference for better, for the better in our community and or their community wherever they should choose to go. But basically my meaning of success would be for my kids, I'm passing on to them a good name and a good start in life.

(Kevin)

Well now my parents' generation is now passing it down to my generation. I'm here, my cousins, a couple of my cousins are here, it's a wonderful idea looking back on the legacy that my grandfather was able to provide but to answer your question, the legacy here is a huge thing to me, it's very important and that's what I strive to continue to pass down to my generation to my kids' generation.

I want to have a tight knit family. I want to continue that, the other thing is I want to see the success of this bank. I want to leave a successful bank that has strong earnings, I want to leave a bank that will be here. We just celebrated our 80th birthday as a bank, I hope in another 80 years the bank is just as strong if not stronger, its more involved in the community, the community is more involved in the bank. Banking to my family is so much stronger than banking to probably 95% of families out there because of the legacy that is here cause of the family that is here. I want to see everything succeed in my life and that's banking and family.

Chapter Summary

The Hankerton family illustrates the importance of having a solid foundation of family values and how such a value system is passed from generation to generation. They also show us the major influence that parents, specifically fathers, have on the career decisions of their sons. Though all participants experienced different jobs within their careers, their paths were similar, including stints in the military and exploring other career options before committing to the family business of community banking. Though bankers, they identified themselves beyond the scope and demonstrated a strong commitment to the community through the workings of the bank. They also displayed a tight-knit family structure, one that values marriage, morals, and teamwork. What was evident was the same set of values were present in each career story and the stories of the first and second generations are embedded in the career identity of the third generation. We also learn there is a considerable amount of admiration that occurred in this family of the parents by their children. Therefore, understand your children are always watching you and how you handle job-related situations, treat others, and make an impact on the community. This ultimately determines, among other things, their decision to become involved in the legacy.

The Hankerton's family career legacy consists of a strong value system, dignity, public service, and involvement of children in the family business. Let's take a more simplified but yet detailed look at the keys to achieve this legacy.

1. Establish a Strong Value System
    a. Have solid family values that are communicated verbally and through actions to the next generation through personal and business interactions and relationships.
    b. Place significance on these values by setting expectations for children educationally, personally, and professionally.
    c. Ensure children and future generations understand the family history, especially of those members who have achieved and/or set forth occupational foundations.
2. Remember the Importance of Dignity
    a. Demonstrate dignity in how you conduct business and manage employees
    b. Treat others with respect as you would your own family members
    c. Maintain a social responsibility to the community with your business
    d. Dignity is not about the amount of money you make but how you think of yourself
    e. Leave a good family name for future generations of your family
3. Commit to Public Service
    a. Exercise compassion in business and relational dealings
    b. Seek ways to serve your community
    c. Uphold your family name in philanthropic and community activities
4. Involve Children in the Family Business
    a. Explain reason for your career choice and your job functions to children
    b. Involve children with small tasks in the family business while they are growing up

c. Be mindful of the words you use about your job around your children and the time your job causes you to spend away from your children

These lessons learned from the Hankerton legacy will be discussed in the last unit of this book, when I present how you can begin to create your own legacy.

CHAPTER 3

"Carve your name on hearts, not tombstones. A legacy is
etched into the minds of others and the stories they share about
you." —Shannon L. Alder

Stories are the composition of our lives in how we come to experience
the world and how the world, through the lives we touch, experience
us. They hold memories rich in history, knowledge, and character
rooted in cultural patterns of values, beliefs, and traditions. Essentially,
stories are the vehicles in which legacies travel from person to person
and generation to generation. Therefore, with each experience,
interaction, and impact, like an avalanche, you are continuously
building and contributing to legacy. Your successes, failures, actions,
and the way you have made people feel and think in forming their
perception of you, are all contained in the told stories that comprise
your legacy.

The goal is to live your life with purpose and meaning so the fruits
of your labor are enjoyed by you and those who come after you.
Essentially, your legacy should live beyond your years and because of
it, society should be better. So the moral of the story this book aspires
to do, is to promote the importance of living an impactful life through
career decisions that provide a living for your family and express
compassion for your community. This type of legacy is demonstrated
through the family career legacies in the form of career stories told by

active family members in their family legacies. The next family's story I share is of the Ortiz family, who exemplify how the power of legacy is etched in the minds and hearts through shared stories about a family who has and continues to make a difference in their community.

The Ortiz Family: Legacy of Restauranteurs

The family career legacy of the Ortiz's is told from the perspective of Melissa, a fourth generation owner of La Cocina, a family-owned and operated Mexican restaurant that has been a staple in the town of Bruce Bluffs for over 35 years. Besides the restaurant, the Ortiz family has its roots in Bruce Bluffs with a history of service, social activism, education, community, and entrepreneurship extending back to 1898 with the arrival of Carlos Ortiz, Melissa's great grandfather. The family is well-known in the City of Bruce Bluffs through their restaurant and the accomplishments of various family members, which include: a wardrobe designer for the late singer, Selena; political and social advocates who were instrumental in the establishment of schools and churches in the Bruce Bluffs Hispanic community; and a host of adult educators, attorneys, philanthropists, and business owners. Figure 3 displays the family tree of Melissa and her family of restaurateurs.

Historic Family Background

As one of the first Mexicans to settle in Bruce Bluffs, a town where Hispanics once only stayed seasonally for agricultural work, Carlos began cooking Mexican dishes for locals, laborers, and travelers before opening his own restaurant. It was not until the late 1930's, mainly 1940's when the growth of Hispanics accelerated in Bruce Bluffs with many of the laborers (many who did not speak English) settling-in there, and forming their own community. During this time, members of the Ortiz family became heavily involved with helping the growing Mexican community economically, politically, spiritually, and educationally. Often times, they were translating documents and conversations for Spanish speakers who wanted to become U.S. citizens.

This legacy of community spans from 1898 until the present, with many key players who are nameless but recognized for their careers and career influence in the formation and continuity of this family career legacy and its rich history. The Ortiz family and La Cocina have received numerous awards from Bruce Bluffs as documented in news articles dated back to the 1970's. Elements of the family's history are documented in the town library; however, much of the information is difficult to locate as events prior to the 1950's (the beginning of the civil rights era in America) that involved marginalized groups, were not written about because of the level of racial discrimination during that time period. The family has since been written about multiple times, as displayed on the wall in their restaurant, and a summary of their history is proudly printed on each of their menus. The Ortiz's most recent recognition is in the form of the Hispanic-Owned Business Community Impact Award, one which the family felt was well-overdue, given their 100 plus years of service in the Bruce Bluffs area.

Fourth Generation

The interview with Melissa Ortiz was a pleasant one. I had received her contact information from a colleague who went to high school with her and had maintained a relationship. Melissa had a bubbly, yet no nonsense personality. When I arrived at the restaurant on a Wednesday afternoon, she immediately motioned me to a table near the bar area where the interview was conducted. One of the things that stood out in the interview was a statement Melissa made a couple of times that was an inadvertent summary of her family background, "Like we always say 'we all came out the hood' we're from the Westside, we all made it! Still makin it, but we made it."

This was evident as during the interview at the restaurant, Melissa's grandfather was sitting at a table next to us reading a newspaper and visiting with a friend. He seemed to be in his 80's, he was olive-skinned with green eyes and white hair, dressed conservatively in a plaid shirt and khaki pants. The restaurant was business as usual as customers seated themselves and staff took their orders with a familiar smile. Her grandfather's friend had on pants and a jacket and they did not seem to talk much, but were present in each other's company like two old friends meeting in the park at their usual time, speaking to each other only when they had something to say. At times, her grandfather would hold up his glass for someone to refill his Coke. During the interview, Melissa's youngest uncle came in the restaurant, very peppy, greeting her with a simple hello and addressing his father with a handshake and

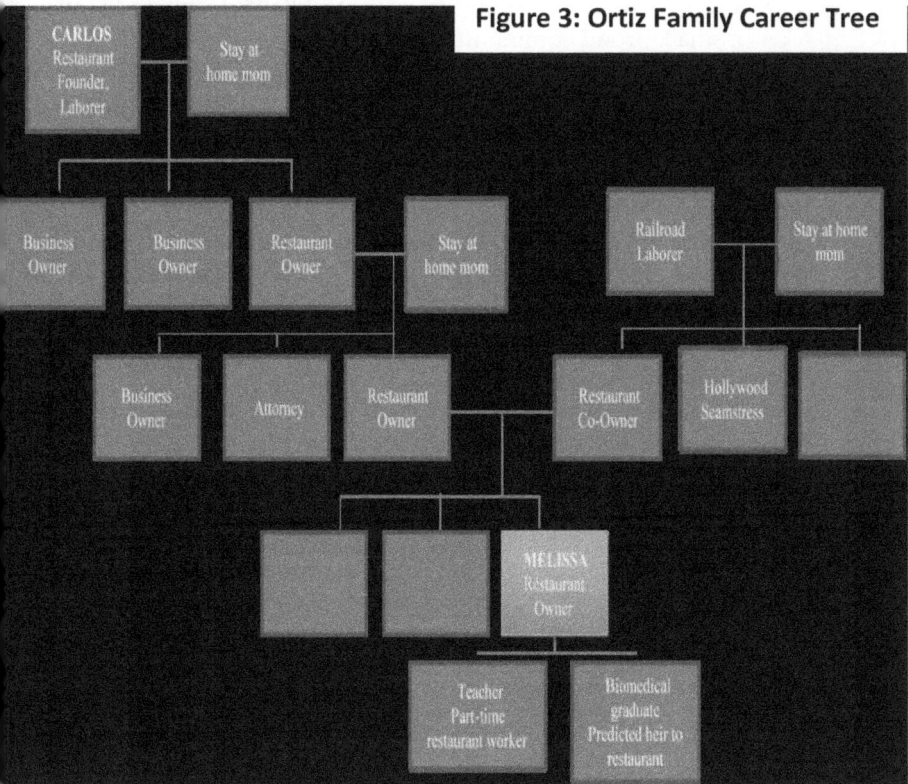

Figure 3: Ortiz Family Career Tree

a loud "Hey bro!" as he went to his regular seat at the bar to watch the FIFA World Cup. The vibe in the restaurant seemed to be familiar, as everyone seemed at home. Above the register, family pictures and multiple article cutouts adorned the warm-colored walls. Announcements of the nearby university were strategically placed near the entrance, to grab the attention of patrons as they waited in line to pay their bill.

Ironically, La Cocina was conveniently located on the corner in historic downtown Bruce Bluffs, an area of town with narrow streets and nostalgic buildings reminiscent of a small, 1800's railroad town, which her great grandfather was among the town's first Mexican settlers in 1898. According to City of Bruce Bluffs' website, Bruce Bluffs, a small-town stop on the railway system, flourished into a popular center for business and trade some 140 years ago and remains today a small, proud community, rich in history.

Named after the nephew of a pioneer considered the "Father of [the state]" for his efforts in the colonization of the state, Bruce Bluffs was incorporated as a city in 1871 and was home to a large number of European immigrants escaping local cotton farms to start their own businesses. During this time, many Mexican immigrants would pass through the town on their way to work in cotton districts and few would settle in the town at that time. However, according to the town's newspaper article in the 1970's and the Ortiz's family history, in the late 1800's, Bruce Bluffs saw a 6'1 tall, young railroad worker, with a signature large sombrero, named Carlos Ortiz. The town paper, many years later, recalled him as one of the first Hispanic settlers (his family counters he was the first Mexican settler) who had brought rich history to Bruce Bluffs through his weekend gatherings for Sunday dinner of serving chicken, rice and beans, vegetables, and tortillas as the children played, the adults socialized, and the elders told stories.

FAMILY BEGINNINGS

Melissa recalled the beginnings of her family as it related to the restaurant.

My grandma and grandpa they were the first Hispanics in this community, yeah they came in the first settlers in Bruce Bluffs. I don't remember them. Well I remember my grandma, she passed away when she was 95 years old. She still smoked Camel cigarettes and she was blind. Yeah she was real tough. "About grandpa, he was the first one to open up a Mexican restaurant right down the corner there by the railroad track" (stated her uncle who later joined the interview for a brief three minutes).

And uh my great grandfather and my grandfather, let's see my grandfather and his brothers, they were fluent in both English and Spanish and uh a lot of the immigrants that would come to town, they would tutor them and help them get their citizenship. They've done a few stories about my grandfather and my great uncle; I think it's at the Library. My great uncle named that, the Cortez school, when discrimination, [was prevalent in the town] it's still there.

She recounted a specific childhood experience of racial discrimination that was common in Bruce Bluffs at the time.

I remember in 1978 and I was in the 5th grade, Mr. Adams, he said 'okay the nurse is coming in and if she calls your name out, it's a new procedure then she'll check you off'. And this was in the classroom in front of all the other students, they were checking hair for lice, and only the Hispanic people were called. By the end of the day, my great uncle, my grandfather, my dad, all the people that were strong leaders, the movers and the shakers in the Hispanic community, they didn't appreciate that one bit. I mean they went... next thing you know they apologized, I mean the damage was done, you know, but it was just a lot of ...that gave my family more fuel, more fuel to show the community that 'we're not trash, we're not dirt'. I'm just proud, we're real proud of our family name.

This example provides a background of understanding the Ortiz family legacy and their tenacity but also illustrates how experiences have led to the construction of the family legacy, value system, and beliefs.

PERSONAL BEGINNINGS

As a female growing up back in the day, the men, the elders would always focus and concentrate on the boys, the young men of the family, my cousins, the males. The women were taught, you know, we're supposed to get married and have the kids and keep the house. They never took us under their wings and gave us that push or you know as a female "you can do this".

Back then I never really thought about a career. Through it all, I had admiration for my mother. My mother has always been a very kind and loving woman, hardworking just always ready to help and just real patient. And just to see the struggles she's been through, her father at the age of 30 became a quadriplegic. He had worked for the railroad and had gotten and had fallen off the boxcar and that paralyzed him. They were all real young at the time and it was nine brothers and sisters and my grandmother, total. She didn't neglect them but she focused all of her energy 24/7 to my grandfather till the day he died, so all the brothers and sisters had to fend for themselves and help one another. So everyone had a role in the family. My mom was the cook and my aunt, the one that's the seamstress now; she made all of the clothes. When it's all said and done, knowing all the struggles that all the family has gone through and she still, she's still here. She's been having some struggles, dementia is settling in but I admire her because she just never gave up.

FAMILY ENVIRONMENT

My grandparents, my great uncles, and aunts always said "you can do anything you want", we always had positive role models in our family. My family has always been go-getters. They have always been in business of that nature and I had an aunt that did hair and I always looked up to her and I think that's why I went the route that I went towards. But I have uncles and family members that are attorneys and doctors and we are all from the West and yep we were never told 'you can't, you can't, you can't', so like we always say 'we all came out the hood' we're from the Westside, we all made it. Still makin it but we made it you know. They were like me and my first cousins, it's a group of us that are all about the same age, we're like 48 and so we were born and raised on the Westside, and they were the babysitters, my great aunt and uncle. They lived next door, it was two brothers and they lived side by side. And so my parents always worked and they would drop us off.

My grandfather, we couldn't go play until we read the newspaper. He would want us to read the newspaper and wanted us to keep up with current events. And we would say "alright we read it" then he would quiz us on it, so we couldn't get away with not ...so that was like uh, and even to this day we have to have a newspaper.

EXISTENCE OF CAREER INFLUENCES AND ROLE MODELS

Gosh I always admired my grandparents and my great-aunt and uncle and then my mom. My dad had five brothers and they all had scholarships either to a junior college or a university. But it was my dad, was an excellent pitcher and I have customers that come in here and say your dad did this and did that and so I didn't realize how good he was or what he achieved back then until now. And then uh my great uncle retired from A&M and he started up in the chemistry department and by the time it was all said and done, he was head of the department and retired from there, so they leave a mark.

My family has always been very helpful and involved and I do have one that's on my mom's side, my mom's sister now works for Paramount Studios. And how she got her start was when Selena was starting up, and my mother's sister was a seamstress. She was also a band promoter and that's how she got to know Selena, cause she would bring her here. My dad and his brother also owned a dance hall and so they would come to town and so through the years Selena would send my aunt sketches of different outfits and stuff and my aunt would make these uniforms, so whenever Selena died, the producer of the movie wanted, got with her parents and wanted to know who made these outfits. They were like 'it was this lady in Bruce Bluffs, Alexa Martinez'. And so they contacted her, she went and made replicas of all the outfits they wanted for the movie. She's pretty famous within our family and within the community, they know of her too. So it's a lot of neat stuff.

CAREER AMBITIONS

Back then I never really, yeah I never really thought about it. I was pretty much born into the business and so I guess I never thought I would actually come in here and take over but I thought about it in probably high school level when I said I'd always have this to fall back on. Actually, in high school I worked at a department store and like a fried chicken place. I always worked for my mom and dad on the weekends or when they needed me. Then I went to beauty school doing hair. I guess I always wanted to be in the beauty industry. I was a hair stylist and I managed salons for 25 years. Then I came eight years ago and took over running the restaurant.

PRESSURE & SUPPORT

No pressure really, um well cause I'm the go-to person in my family. Well my dad wanted me to go to A&M being in this town and we got a house full of family members that are Huskies. You now when you live in this town you are born a Huskie. There are several family members that could have really made something for themselves but they just settled. And there was another handful and they were pushed and pushed and pushed, you know, and they're very successful and we are all different. But I guess we kind of fed off each other, so we see so-and-so is this and we were kind of like that energy, you know, so it was kind of, it just depended on what was going on at the time.

Well we're a close-knit family; we always encourage and talk about what we can do to be better. We have never been negative, we always been positive and supportive of everything. We got a lot of encouragement and guidance. My parents always worked, they were always busy and it was mainly my grandparents and my great aunt and uncle. We got a lot of encouragement and guidance from them because they were hands on, they were the one. You know and they have always, my grandparents, my great uncles and aunts always said 'you can do anything you want'.

I just always wanted to do makeup and hair and all this stuff and so my dad would always say 'you not going to do all this stuff' and this and that and anyway I ended up being very successful at what I did. So then you know he backed off. But you know they were disappointed and were not discouraging in what I did cause they knew I was a strong woman. I took it to the top.

FAMILY VALUES

To be humble, to be honest, never turn your back on someone in need. My grandparents and my great aunts and uncles that lived side by side, people knew they could go to them for financial help or food. They never turned their back. They showed us not to take anything for granted. Hard work and determination, nobody gonna do it for you, it's all up to you as an individual and so this, all this different types of traits and to be helpful and give back. Gosh let's see, staying humble and giving back pretty much all those and I would say aggressiveness and don't be lazy. Don't waste your life away, don't burn daylight, there's always something to do.

SENSE OF BELONGING AND COMMUNITY

I can remember as a little girl, my grandmother going to her kitchen and getting a grocery bag and putting whatever she had and loading it up and giving it to the lady at the front door. And I've seen my dad, my parents as they started, they had a business you know, a little ways down but then we came here. The mission used to be down the street but they've moved it. Since then my dad would get a lot of the mission people and they would come and they were hungry and he would never turn them down. He would give them a hard time and say 'Ok well go out there and sweep. Here's a broom, you gonna sweep out there and clean this window and I'm gonna feed you' and then they just showed us not to take anything for granted.

My grandfather, his father, my great-uncle a lot of these Hispanic families here in town wouldn't have gotten their citizenship, like I was telling you, they tutored them and they even drove them to [the nearest major city] and they didn't charge them. They would try to pay them but they would tell them 'give the money to the church' cause at that time they were building a Hispanic church because back then there wasn't [one]. I know my grandparents and my great aunt and uncle they were in this community. Being that my great grandfather was one of the first Hispanics in this town.

PIVOTAL AND TURNING POINT EXPERIENCES IN CAREER

Well the whole story on that is, um my mom had, she was diagnosed with lymphoma and my dad had the quadruple bypass but they continued and they didn't let, when my mom was down, my dad stepped up, when my dad was down, my mom stepped up. That's when I came in and helped them and I've seen their illnesses and stuff but they're still here, they're still hanging on. Then it got to the point and they were just gonna shut it down. And we were like 'no, no, no, you can't do that'. So when I made the career change to quit doing what I was doing and came in here fulltime, what helped me was that I have always been in management customer service, so I kinda just, it just worked for me. I guess working with people, you meet all kinds of people. I'm just thankful I'm good with people and I guess the service industry. Coming to work is rough because you never gonna know what's going to happen but it's fun, you know, it's fun.

MAKING MEANING OF CAREER EXPERIENCES

I was actually successful as a hairstylist and working here and keeping up with my household. They tell me that God always puts…you know, God put me where He wanted, you know I have three, two older sisters, one younger sister, well she's 38, 39. I have one sister, she's got $5, she gonna spend $6. My other sister she's still trying to crawl. You know and so I was the one that my parents would come get. When I stepped in I said 'look I'm gonna do this because ya'll can't close this up' and I came in here and they just looked real pleased by it and so, they were glad *that it was me and not the other ones. I've always been the one, don't ever tell me "no", because I'm gonna run with it. I've always been that one, very stubborn, high strung, never can be still, um I gonna… I want it all done yesterday and so I would say I just learned to…I don't know, unless it's just natural.*

Being a Hispanic woman I have always and I'm very hardheaded and stubborn and tomboyish and I'm very rebellious because it was always for the boys. And I would fight them and I would show them that I was better, so I think that kind of gave me, you know, as a woman to prove myself more. Oh yeah, I can get like a man. I will chase a man outside too. They have to stop me and say 'remember you're a girl'; I can get on their level and get competitive with them on pricing. If I don't know it, I'm going to ask questions, so that's how you learn. You know so I'm very high strung but I, you know, now that I think about it, I run that kitchen!

It's a lot but a lot of these women that work here, I take them under my wing and tell them 'don't ever depend on a man, you make something of yourself'. I see a lot of these girls they come in and they don't go to college and they get with a guy and they get pregnant and all that stuff, and I tell them "look"… I just give them words of encouragement. A lot of them will tell me 'oh we look up to you, you're so strong and you're this and you're that', you know. And I say 'you don't have to be ugly and nasty'. You just have to be professional, show them you're smart and they're not gonna look down on you or belittle you and if they do, just keep on, just give them something more to hate you about'. So yeah it's a lot of work trying to fight these men.

My meaning of success is putting your mind to something and doing it and making it happen whether it's something very small or very big. It doesn't have to deal with money but just starting something and finishing it. Don't be a quitter. To me if you finish something you started, don't ever give up. I don't care what it is, always give it your best at whatever you put your mind to.

In making meaning of her career experience, Melissa subconsciously embraces the values and behaviors she saw demonstrated by her family members in their dealings in business and through social activism. Essentially, she models what she observed and incorporated in her own way for the causes that were important to her in her daily interactions with staff. In this way, Melissa is continuing the legacy not only through the family business but the family value system of helping others.

CONTINUANCE OF THE LEGACY

We have a legacy because of our family name. I mean we got four generations of customers coming in here. We've been around a long time and its rare mom and pop restaurants survive. There's a lot of, I mean from where my parents started until now, we've come a long way. There's still so much more to do and so much more to grow. I mean we're not a major corporation. We don't have those dollars or that competition…it's just us. We've come a long way and there's still a long way to go. But day by day it's a struggle and it's a lot of work trying to keep it. I always say this is a monster "the monster" it's still I think, God willing, the next generation after me, hopefully, one of my daughter's will take it to another level, you know. My oldest is a graduate. She teaches at camp elementary and kindergarten, so she helps during the summertime, and my youngest daughter, she's on maternity leave, so she comes in. She got a degree in biomedical science but she, she's more family oriented and she has more pride as well, so I think she gonna be the one to come in and take over. Yeah, I hope, so I can take a break.

Chapter Summary

Melissa's career story is just another addition to the Ortiz family career legacy of running a restaurant that gathers the community together for food, fellowship, and encouragement. As she stated, her family's legacy is in their name, which is representative of their value and belief system that has fueled their career choices. From the beginning of a laborer who had the notion to feed others, the legacy of the Ortiz family lives on through the restaurant. La Cocina, the heartbeat of the family, exemplifies its beginnings and continues to serve the community. In its fourth generation, Melissa plans to ensure it remains a pillar in the community under the control of the fifth generation.

The Ortiz family career legacy provides us with these five key points:

1. Provide encouragement and guidance for future generations.
    a. Despite their career decisions, be encouraging of their dreams and aspirations and provide guidance where necessary.

2. Establish a tight-knit family.
    a. Do family activities together and spend time with family. Ensure children of same ages interact with each other, visit other family members, and hold regular family events, like Sunday dinners or monthly, quarterly gatherings.
    b. Share stories about family history and other members of your family and their accomplishments.
3. Have a family first mentality.
    a. Uphold the family name and reputation by becoming involved in family activities and exude family values in your own activities and careers.
        i. Set expectations of what it means to be a member of your family through community involvement, careers, and values. Demonstrate these values and expectations.
    b. Remember the values and let that guide your career decisions and community involvement.
4. Be socially aware and active.
    a. Get your children involved to understand current events.
    b. Make it a mission to help others in need, including family members, to progress your community and the communities you serve and who support your business. Embrace others into your family.
5. Be persistent in creating your legacy and encourage others to be go-getters.

CHAPTER 4

"It doesn't matter what you do...so long as you change
something from the way it was before you touched it into
something that's like you after you take your hands away."
--Ray Bradbury

Legacy is more of what you do and less of what you inherit. Sure, our
families provide us, hopefully, with the foundational values and tools
to succeed in life but it is what we do with those resources that really
matters. Some of us begin life with a greater advantage than others;
being born into or given finances, networks, shelter, and opportunities.
All the while, there are others of us who will essentially have to turn
lemons into lemonade to obtain positive success. The fact of the
matter, regardless of the inheritance or lack thereof, the charge is still
the same. You must make the world a better place for future
generations; otherwise, we will eventually diminish. Because you were
born into a rut, does not mean you deserve to remain there and because
you were born into enough money to make your grandchildren
wealthy, does not mean your work is done. Luke 12:48 tells us "For
unto whomsoever much is given, of him shall be much required: and
to whom men have committed much, of him they will ask the more";
ergo, the more you have the more you are expected to do and give.

So I present to you a family career legacy that embodies this
generative expectation. The Herrera family has a career legacy of

farming that spawned a career legacy of community banking. Though the career changes, the values remain the same, as we have discussed and seen demonstrated in the legacies in the previous chapters of this book. What is unique about the Herrera's is their modest beginnings becomes the motivation for greater provision for future generations and this provision supersedes societal suppression to create greater opportunities for future generations of Herrera's and Hispanics native to the area.

The Herrera Family: A Legacy of Community Banking

This story details the family career legacy (Figure 4) of the Herrera's, a family of community bankers in a north-central, southwestern town of Caracalla. This story is told from the perspective of Patty, a third generation CEO at Pinnacle Bank, a community bank founded by her grandfather, Armando and taken over by her father, Alonzo, who served as president and CEO. Upon retiring, Alonzo passed the torch to Patty, who became bank president at 23 years old and now serves as CEO and Board Chairman.

This family's modest beginnings stem back to Armando's upbringing on a fourth generation farm, where his persistence and intellect afforded him the opportunity for higher education. After a pivotal experience of being denied a bank loan because of his ethnicity, he set out to establish what is now known as Pinnacle Bank. Throughout the years, he enlisted the help of the community and family to not only found the bank but manage its operations. Alonzo, continued the legacy of community by doing the same family enlisting demonstrated by his father after Armando wanted to return to law. Then after two decades of running the bank, Alonzo's preparation of his protégé for leadership was not in vain, as Patty graduating from college, decided it was time for her to make an impact on the community. And home was where she knew she could.

Coming back home to help the community was the common thread between the three as they all had opportunities to succeed elsewhere in larger cities. Their commitment to growth and impact in their community, compassion, desire for social justice, and family values of hard work, integrity, and passion created and maintained a financial institution that exemplifies their heart for people, family, and the future.

Though Armando and Alonzo are still alive and there are several other members of the family who work at the bank, Patty was the only one available for interviewing via Skype. Though I could only interact with her over the Internet, I found her demeanor pleasant and reserved. She appeared to be in her late 30's to early 40's, brown hair, and wearing a khaki collared shirt. This family career legacy is told from Patty's perspective with external documents that corroborate and add to her narrative to provide a holistic understanding of her career story.

Pinnacle Bank's website offers a great quote by Patty that provides insight into this family career legacy.

Giving back to our community is who and what Pinnacle Bank is all about. Caracalla is my home and I believe in the power of community to make a difference for future generations. For me, our giving program is not just about money, it is about being a proactive leader in making our community a better place to live and work. This takes resources of many kinds including our time, getting involved, rolling up our sleeves and working hard to make a difference.

Figure 4: Herrera Family Career Tree

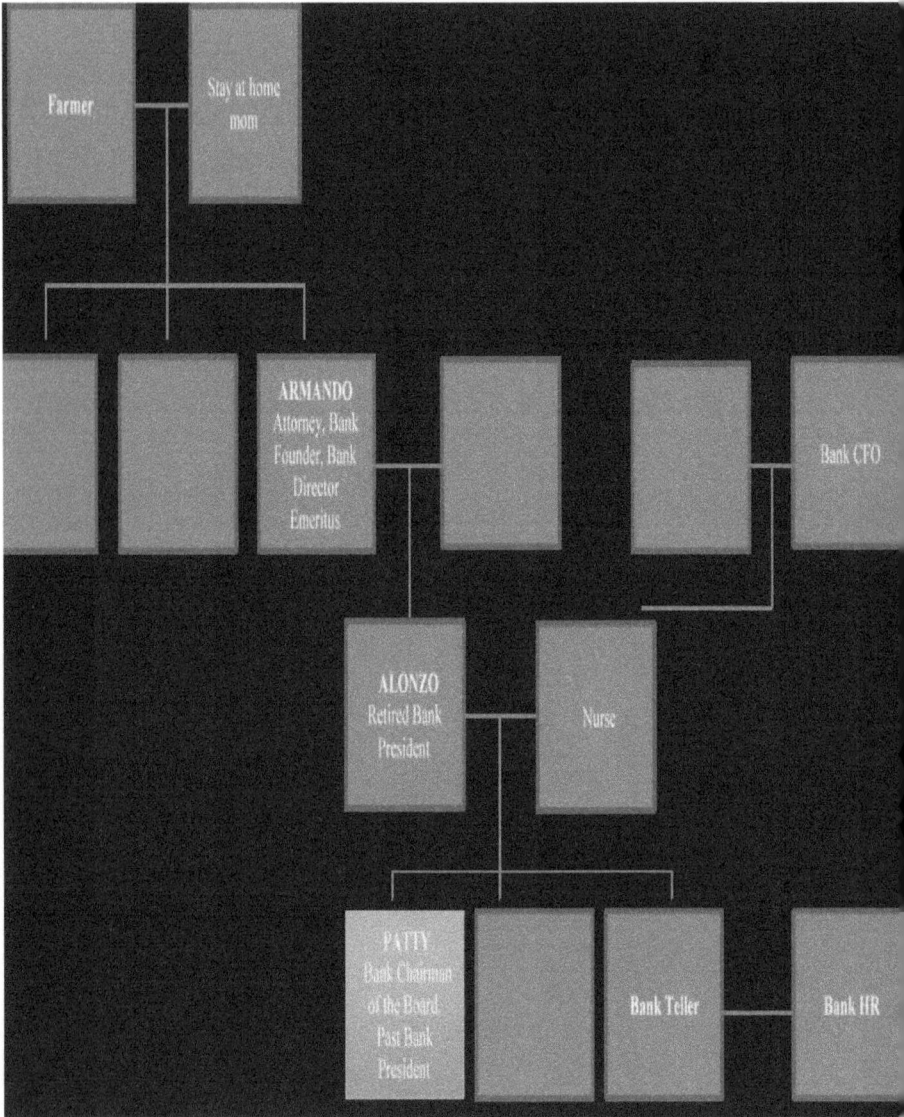

First Generation

The town of Caracalla is one full of rich heritage that dates back to over 6,000 years as a travel destination for Nomadic hunters and gatherers. It is quietly known for being a modern town with a healthy culture scene, attracting artists of all genres to its mountainous views and multiple nationally registered historic sites. The town, with a population of 5,710 (52% Hispanic and 40% White population), suffers from 23% of its residents under the poverty line and limited higher education opportunities. Though a predominantly Hispanic town, the City of Caracalla has not always availed equal opportunities for its majority residents.

Patty recalled her family's legacy beginnings to her grandfather Armando Herrera who grew up in Caracalla as a fourth generation farmer, producing enough food for the family and herding sheep.

FAMILY BEGINNINGS

It's a great story. So my grandfather is originally from this community within the northern part of the state and put himself through law school, after serving in the Navy and Merchant Marines. He decided he wanted to come back to help the Hispanic community here. At that time, a majority minority community of course was Hispanic, but the majority of the businesses were owned and operated by the Anglo community.

This was in the late 1950's and early 1960's, when discrimination on every level was rampant in the United States and several groups and individuals were emerging to protect and promote civil rights and racial equality for all ethnic groups.

He felt that his people, his community, their needs were not being represented or met. In fact when he moved back to Caracalla, he applied for a $500 loan to get his law practice started and could not get that money. It made him so mad that he came up with this idea to start his own bank. He's just that kind of determined individual that 'if someone's not going to help me do it, I'm going to do it my own way'. Sure enough it took him over 10 years to get the charter, he did not have the money, did not have the experience, so he put together a group of over 300 people that provided the initial capital for the bank.

He made numerous applications to the FDIC to get the charter and it wasn't until he randomly got appointed to a small business administration committee in the

Nixon administration that he made a connection to somebody who knew somebody that could help him get this charter. It was no easy thing and the first 10 years of the bank were very rocky; they had a difficult time. Nobody knew what they were doing; they were really making it up as they went along. But they were determined and they stuck with it and my dad came back into the bank, the bank was started in 1969, and my dad came into the bank in 1978.

Armando founded Pinnacle Bank with the principle to "serve all the people, cultures, and languages of the Caracalla County community". According to a local newspaper, community banks are "located in small towns, suburbia and big-city neighborhoods, our nation's nearly 7,000 community banks help fuel local economies throughout America by lending to small businesses, helping local residents and families purchase homes, finance college and build solid financial futures". Throughout the years, the Herrera's have established a holding company and as a family, have ownership of all outstanding stock of Pinnacle Bank, making it a minority owned financial institution, which is one of few in the United States.

Second Generation

Patty's father, Alonzo, gained banking experience by working at his father's bank throughout the years, since its inception and through external banking positions. In 1978, after serving as a branch manager at a different bank in another neighboring city, he returned to work at Pinnacle on a full-time basis.

The funny part of the story is that he spent a couple of years doing that, his mother-in-law, my mom's mom, was an accountant and my dad was not trained in business. He was really doing this to help his dad make it work. And he, struggling with some of the financial side of things and just finding somebody he could trust to really get things on the solid ground, he knew an accountant. He literally hired his mother-in-law to become the CFO of the bank and the two of them were the ones that took the place to a whole another level. So it's actually both sides of my family that were involved.

It was under his leadership that Pinnacle's shaky start evolved to one of the largest Hispanic owned corporations in the United States, the seventh best small business to work for in the state and "Top Workplace" in 2013.

Another big thing, my mom was very involved in the bank, she was the HR director while my dad was president and CEO.

Third Generation

I had, growing up as a teenager, I think starting at the age of 13. I started working at the bank, whether it was answering phones, sorting mail, random projects, copying, you know the typical summer intern, that was my job. I think my earlier years I wanted to be a teacher, there was a time when my mom was doing some of her work [as a nurse], I thought that would be cool. I've always loved babies and being around babies, through elementary and middle school years. In high school years the concept of finance and business and working with numbers became of interest to me. And politics became of interest to me which was weird because I was an incredibly shy child. I was intrigued with studying leaders and what the realm of politics and what somebody can do to find a sense of common ground to bring people together. That became more my aspirations that led to a degree in political science and economics that led down that path. But I was all over the board as a kid. (laughs)

EXISTENCE OF CAREER INFLUENCES AND ROLE MODELS

You know, my dad certainly was [an influence], so was my mother because she was working. My dad would leave early in the morning and come home late at night. The amount of time spent with him was not as much but I was always very intrigued with what he was doing and how he was involved in the community and that certainly started a lot for me. My mom was working and raising the three of us and that was certainly part of me seeing someone who could be a career woman and certainly raise kids.

My grandmother, who was the CFO, was also a role model. She was the pioneer in terms of being a strong female in the banking business; even now it's still male dominated, so to see her be involved and work at that national (inaudible) association. Whenever there was a problem, she was the one who got in to dig deeper

75

with some of the issues and doing some great problem solving. She was that very strong female role model that helped me with thinking that at the ripe age of 23... So seeing all three of them in their unique approaches I think is a lot of reason I'm incredibly strong and intimidating. I knew in watching what I had learned from them that I could do this and I could figure it out.

PRESSURE & SUPPORT

No, I mean my dad was always open and would say "I only want you to do this, if this is something you want to do". I have to admit at the same time, coming into this, this family legacy is cool, there's so much here that means so much to me as an individual that the employees that we have that remind me of my family. So many of them I grew up around them as a kid, and then worked for them and came in as their boss. So in a pressure sense, I did have some sense of wanting to see that continue. And I was really the only one who could do that. I couldn't necessarily see one of my brothers wanting to take on that role in that level of necessity and so for me it was not necessarily the pressure of wanting or feeling that I had to come into the bank, for me was the question of do I want to play a role in the continuation of this legacy.

FAMILY VALUES

There was a comment always said around our house "always do the right thing", not the easy thing but the right thing and that has been a (inaudible) that when I'm challenged with the decision that is the right thing to do and that has guided me through so many difficult decisions. [Also], work ethic, passion, integrity, sense of compassion and caring to treat business as not just it's our livelihood or net worth.

MAKING MEANING OF CAREER EXPERIENCES

In college I did some of the traditional work study, work in the admissions office, you know those types of things. But in terms of being a real job, this is the only real job I've ever had. I started training as a teller, summers during college I ran a branch. I had different opportunities to work different positions in the bank. In my senior year of college I didn't necessarily think I would come back immediately. In fact, I was a political science and economics major, I took several accounting classes. I knew that business finance was a general path I wanted to go down but I thought maybe I would stay in the city awhile and explore some options there. So I went through the traditional recruiting route and got a couple of job offers to do your classic consulting or different things right out of college.

It was possibly March of my senior year thinking okay this could possibly be fun and could be interesting and at the same time and evaluating what kind of impact I was going to make in the world. Working in a cubicle? But what was that going to do for me or anyone else around me? Um and for me it came down to knowing this is an opportunity. I can jump into this and if I didn't try it, how was I going to know that it was something I wanted to do? The really underlying part of it was coming to a point in my life where I really started thinking what difference am I going to make out there and how am I going to get an impact to be able to do that. And coming back to a community bank that had a history of being very engaged in the community where I could really design the job and my impact the way I wanted to, the minute I hit the ground. So that for me was really what made the decision to come back here.

That's what I think is my motivator for coming back so quickly, cause I need to know that this is something that I feel comfortable doing. Does it give me the satisfaction? If it really was something that I wanted to do or not, maybe I needed to know that sooner than later than just decide on what next step to take.

So I spent the next two years literally working side by side with my dad continuing to train in different areas and at the age of 23, I took over as president of the $100 million bank because he was really ready to go onto the next step. [He] felt like if I was going to do this I needed to do it and he didn't want to stand in my way. And so it was a rather quick path but one in which I had the opportunity. In the course of about 10 years, I'll be coming in and out and having the opportunity to work in just about every position of the bank, even though I was only about 23, I had that experience and was able to do that at that point.

Patty's career as president and now CEO and chairman of the board for Pinnacle Bank has continued the family's precedence. Her most recent accomplishment has been her election as vice chairman of the Independent Community Bankers of America (ICBA), vice chairman of the Federal Delegate Board, member on the Bank Education Committee, past chairman of the Minority Bank Council and vice chairman of the Lending Committee, current service on the Federal Reserve Community Depository Institutions Advisory Council, and has served on the Federal Reserve Community Depositor

Institution Advisory Council, and has met with President Obama to discuss lending practices and regulatory reform.

SENSE OF COMMUNITY AND BELONGING

The Herrera family believes in being involved in the community and investing in youth. They also have an entrepreneur award named after Armando who said, "We are committed to and care deeply for our customers, our neighbors and our community".

Sense of compassion and caring to treat business as not just it's our livelihood or net worth it's a lot that impacts us as a family and it is so much more than that. It is a group of individuals that have given their life to this organization in terms of being so dedicated and so loyal that it is a family, an extended family. Whether it's being there in the tough times or the happy times and the good times, to celebrate to mourn, to ascend, we do whatever we can to help take care of that group and know that that's just what we do and it makes being here a real special place to be.

And then whether it's the local Habitat for Humanity or gathering food for individuals, there's a lot to do in the schools. That's another part and obviously as a mother of two young kids, I'm involved in schools and what I do ranges in PTA and providing resources and at times providing political to individuals struggling here, I do a lot there as well.

Patty's involvement with the bank has allowed her to extend her philanthropic efforts that build from the values and accomplishments of her grandfather, mother, father, and grandmother. Her philanthropy extends to president and co-founder of a nonprofit focused on helping first-generation college students, board member and past-president of the State Birth Center, and accolades such as: Caracalla Citizen of the Year 2009 and the Governor's Award for outstanding women.

CONTINUANCE OF THE LEGACY

I think the stuff that I picked up that I can trace back maybe to some of their interest overtime; for example, my parents instituted a great scholarship program for local high school graduates. That had always been something that they themselves were very involved and engaged with and so I've certainly continued that. One of the first things I did when I came back to Caracalla was to work with another person and start a nonprofit that provides one-on-one college counseling, support, and services of people of any age. So kind of taking that concept to fund that education a step further, really seeing the need, we're a rural community and a school that didn't have a lot, the counselors are the discipliners and not the college counselors.

So we started that six years ago and it's still going very strong in this community. So I certainly took their base and that interest and certainly helped grow it. So this literally, and I can tell you there are other several family members that are involved in the bank. My youngest brother is a loan officer and he's active in management and we work incredibly well together. I love that he is here with me. And his wife also works with us. She's in our HR area; she helps with our community development and organization development, the training, those sorts of things. So the three of us are actively involved.

My mom prior to coming to the organization was a nurse and a midwife before that, so she had a lot of connections with the nurses and community in Caracalla and the bank actually helped fund the construction of a birthing center here in Caracalla. They had done that when I had my children. I worked with the midwife and became in engaged in that direction and I've been doing that for about nine years now. So there is definitely some similar interests that they have started that now I've continued in my own way.

For my children, I would hope to leave a strong basis for them to be able to make a decision for them to do what I did in terms of knowing all the good, bad, and ugly of what it is we do within this organization and do that in a way they're able to make a decision for themselves whether or not this is something that they want to spend time doing or not. And continue to build it in such a way that hopefully whether or not they themselves wanted to work here that this organization would continue on strong, vibrant and with many options for different leaders and ways it could be operated. So that it really is and continues strong that they learn the lessons of what this place does and how it does it that they get a sense of what it takes to make it happen and the importance of giving back. That whatever it is that they do, they have that sense of responsibility to turn it back around to be, um, to just have the sense to give back. I'm having a hard time articulating that, hopefully that makes sense.

Regarding Pinnacle, I would like see it on this continued path of steady growth and success. As a community bank one thing we say is there is steady growth that we incrementally continue to grow the customer bank, to grow our skillset, to enhance what we do that we just continue on that same trajectory of growth and not just in the sense of business accounts. And people that we are serving, everyone in the organization builds in what it's able to do and with that comes the ability to continue to support the community and be that pillar within the community. We continue to grow that strength and operate within a realm that encourages community banks in their unique structure and aspiration and role within the community.

I want to be remembered for helping make this organization a better place to live and work and for all the staff's needs. That I play even a small role in helping to better somebody's life through this community and organization and student procedure to be there to help wherever I can and continue to be remembered for being the person that did whatever she could, when she could, is what I hope folks would remember.

To me legacy is a connection to the past and a vision for the future that is here because someone believed that this community needed its own community bank. It needed its own organization that would pull its own community resources that would leverage people that would buy their homes, build their businesses, to grow the community. So for me it's that connection and that path and also knowing that there's a vision for continued growth for positive things to happen in the future. Yes, the legacy they left me was this opportunity to take what they had built and made so strong and to give me the opportunity to put my own stamp, my own vision, my own thoughts on it, and carry it in the future.

Patty's grandfather, Armando, though well into his 80's, is a retired attorney, and still considered a staple in the Caracalla community. In 2011, he was selected by the City mayor to pursue litigation for a land grant on behalf of Caracalla. Even at the age of 84, Armando was still on call to fight for the rights of others. This trickles down to Patty's insistence of seeking a career that will give her the opportunity to make an impact in the community and continue the legacy of growth of the bank and community.

Alonzo held the position of CEO for 20 years and when he relinquished his position to Patty, he stated "She was balancing our checkbook when she was in the sixth grade" and her grandfather said in her current position, "She's beyond comparison". In conclusion, Patty added, she hoped the name Herrera has the legacy with a reputation of "determination, hard work, commitment, and sense of purpose of being and that overwhelming generosity and desire to do good".

Chapter Summary

Making an impact by invoking communal change was the major take away from the Herrera Family. Their legacy built on determination, commitment to growth, and family involvement all contributed to their passion for social justice for their community. From the tenacity of Armando to ensure equality for bank loans, the Herrera family has continued to involve family in business ventures and philanthropy. Each of the three generations has incorporated their unique perspective into the family business to advance the family career legacy. Through their family values and community involvement, the Herrera's legacy has improved the lives of many in their community, giving hope and equal opportunity to those less fortunate.

Their legacy teaches us the following:

1. Involve family in career and community efforts.
   a. Get children involved in the family business and give them tasks to teach them responsibility and soft skills.
   b. Be committed to growth and development for future generations and demonstrate to children the importance of community and family.
2. Share family history.
   a. Share childhood and professional/career stories with children about your experiences and those of past generations. These stories pass along family values and also provide a connection with past and future.
3. Become change agents.
   a. Think about how you can make your community and world better and devise a plan to do so.
   b. Never stop fighting for social justice and begin to build a solid network/alliance to help advance social issues.

CHAPTER 5

"The choices we make about the lives we live determine the kinds of legacies we leave." Tavis Smiley

Life is full of choices. The goal of this book is to provide options and inspiration to make different choices in how you can live a life that leaves a positive legacy for you and your family. In creating or building a legacy, we must begin to think about the choices we make in our careers and also how we chose to deal with the "hand we are dealt", if you will. Understanding our current situation and the dynamics of our physical and social environments is key to our decision making. This can be an advantage and also a limitation in the available resources and the barriers we have to overcome; however, no matter our circumstances, we all have a choice. If we believe in ourselves and begin to look ahead instead of behind and presently, we can overcome any obstacle. I encourage you to begin to make the choices of who you will surround yourself with, who will you mentor or let mentor you, who will be your support system and network, what moral and belief compass will you subscribe to, how will you make a difference, and how will you make the best of your current situation?

This next family I will introduce you to is a great example of how to use your environment to your advantage. The Jones family is building a remarkable legacy from their patriarch's entrepreneurial vision, which stems from limited resources due to racial segregation.

This family's career legacy teaches the importance of having a strong community, support system, and spiritual compass. You will have a better understanding of what it is to have a calling as your career. Additionally, you will further see how career legacies affect future generations and how those different generations can contribute their individual careers to the overall legacy of the family.

The Jones Family: Legacy of Community Service

The Jones family is one of different beginnings than most family career legacies. The patriarch was not part of a family legacy but one with a supportive family environment and a quest for opportunity that allowed him to create a legacy through his career accomplishments. It is through his legacy and quest to extend his legacy to include his son that he actually replicates the same supportive environment he experienced and allows his career legacy to perpetuate his sons' career aspirations. Together, father and sons, have created a family career legacy they hope will sustain to the third generation based on reputation, regardless of actual career. Essentially, the Jones family career legacy (Figure 5) is based on a legacy of service to the community through career and not on a followed career path.

This family career legacy is told from the perspective of Richey Donovan Jones (Richey Don), a legendary radio disc jockey and music promoter turned funeral home owner and his sons Todd and Jordan, dedicated morticians at the family owned funeral home, Jones & Sons. The story of the Jones' illustrates the power of the familial influence on career decisions and the development of career identity (how a person perceives viable career options based on their experiences, skillsets, interests, and motivations) in job selections.

The ways of the 21st century show us that jobs are passé because jobs consist of the many duties and opportunities one will have in their career and how they identify themselves, or their career identity, is the actual indicator of their profession. Richey Don, a self-proclaimed businessman, finds comfort in being known as a disc jockey (DJ).

There is no doubt that he is, but he is a DJ who happens to be in the funeral business as well. This is the postmodern career world we live in now. People have many jobs they perform in their career and they all contribute to the legacy they have maintained; their career portfolio. The career stories of this family career legacy begins with Richey Don's and ends with Todd and Jordan's and their plan to continue the legacy started by their father.

First Generation

Figure 5: Jones Family Career Tree

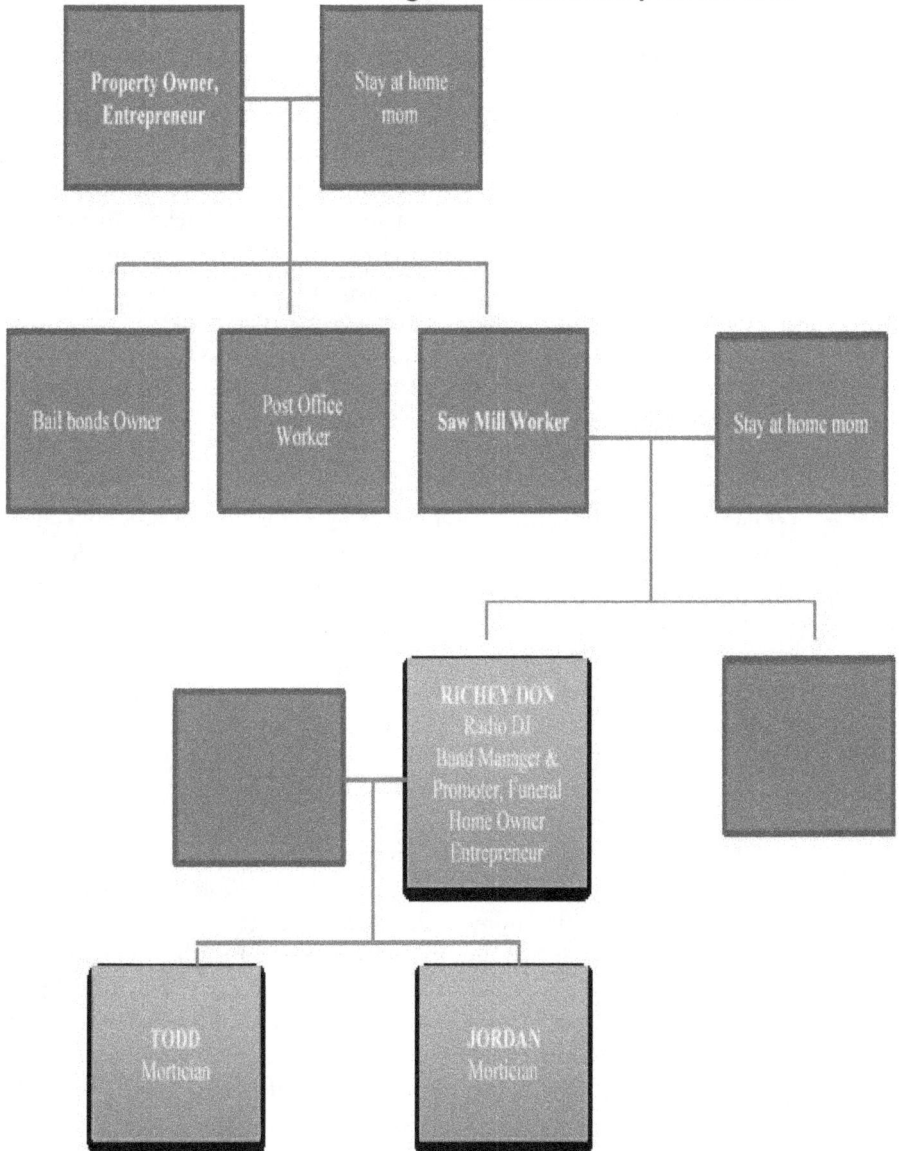

Property Owner, Entrepreneur

Stay at home mom

Bail bonds Owner

Post Office Worker

Saw Mill Worker

Stay at home mom

RICHEY DON
Radio DJ
Band Manager &
Promoter, Funeral
Home Owner
Entrepreneur

TODD
Mortician

JORDAN
Mortician

Richey Don grew up in small southern town in the United States in the1930's, a time when it was common to drink water from a well, 15 cents fed his family of four at the locally-owned grocer, and segregation was the way of life. Many Blacks in these areas often moved town to town in search for employment opportunities in manufacturing plants and as agricultural laborers, with some settling in major cities for steady employment and greater educational, commercial, professional, and social opportunities. One of the cities that became attractive to many Black small town residents, was Darton, a growing city known for its good race relations (for a southern city) and one of the best opportunities for life and career in the south for Blacks. In fact, in many ways Darton's Black community was like its own city; having rich, middle-class, and lower class Blacks and Black owned businesses, establishments, professional organizations, newspapers, hospitals, theaters, parks, beauty salons, and libraries in its own areas of town. The Darton Black community thrived and ranked among the top cities with successful Black communities in the nation.

In the 1960's , Avalon Heights, a Black area in Darton became the greatest concentration of Black businesses and for nearly 30 years, remained a culture center for Darton area Blacks. Avalon Heights attracted entrepreneurs and thrill-seekers from all over the U.S. as it quickly rose to the top as one of the great entertainment centers for Blacks. Avalon Heights' large Black population caused it to be a major attraction to Black entertainers; thus, requiring the need for Black DJs and promoters to connect and service the city's population and entertainment needs.

RICHEY DON'S STORY

One of those pioneers is Richey Don, the man who, self-proclaimed, "brought a mountain of soul to Darton." Richey, a tall man with a deep commanding voice, who often refers to himself in the third person, has a personality that is as large as his physicality. He is known for his great sense of humor and ability to connect with people. A great storyteller, in his autobiography, Richey accounts his reputation of being the life of the party, recalling how others expected a good time with him because he would bring the girls, drinks, and fun. Richey was also known for his community involvement, often putting on benefit concerts, launching careers of others, and promoting Black businesses, and engaging in community activities and service.

Throughout his legendary career, he has received national recognition for his radio career and for being the most popular DJ in Darton Black media. "In the world of black [Darton] radio, [Richey] is a god". Other journalists declared "He [Richey] was one of the most influential disc jockeys of his era" and "He was one of the people who made [Darton]...a fountainhead of black popular music." In essence, as Richey stated it from the recollection of others, "Richey Donovan is the man!" A man who wants to be known for bringing a "mountain of soul to Darton," which was a family dialogue and infamous opening to his radio show in the 1960's. The dialogue is as follows:

Richey Don, tell us your story. When did you come to Darton and why? This is my story. Last night as I tried to sleep, it seemed I could hear voices. These voices kept telling me, 'Richey Don, steal away and carry a mountain of soul to Darton.' Over and over again I kept hearing the same voices. 'Richey Don, steal away and carry a mountain of soul to Darton.' Over and over again I kept hearing those voices. So I called my mother and I kissed her goodbye. I called my father in and shook his hand. As I walked out the door with my bags in my hand, I knelt down and kissed my little sister. Then I began the long, lonesome journey to carry a mountain of soul to Darton because I could not ignore those voices. Over and over again I kept hearing those same voices. 'Richey Don, steal away and carry a mountain of soul to Darton.' Have mercy, have mercy. So here I am Darton! Here I am, Darton! I've brought a mountain of soul to this city. Have mercy, have mercy.

A fitting introduction for the man whose career legacy is the center and foundation of this family career legacy. On a sunny March day, I paid a visit to this Darton icon at his office at the family's business, Jones & Sons Funeral Home. The entrance was a typical glass double door with a pull handle; however, a thick, burgundy curtain draped the inside of the door, which signified funeral. After opening the door, I was pleasantly surprised with the décor that looked more like a home instead of a funeral home. The smell of potpourri filled the air, flowered wallpaper bordered the walls, rose colored plush carpet draped the steps, and gold accessories served as accents for the décor. To my left, was a wooden desk where someone greeted me and told me to take the stairs, make a left at the top and go straight back and I would see Richey Don in his office.

As I got to the top of the steps, I was taken aback by the tremendous space in this building and how much it did not look like a funeral home. On the walls was a collage of at least 100 pictures in frames covering the four walls; similar to a wall of fame, especially like those at restaurants where the owner takes pictures with celebrities who have visited the establishment. I became in awe as I saw pictures of the Jackson 5, James Brown, Muhammad Ali, and other legendary people with the same man with an afro and a smile so big, it could light up a room. I continued to follow the directions and as I approached the only open door, I was greeted by Richey Don, the constant smile in those pictures, but now he was more distinguished. He stood about 6'3, with glasses and a low cut hair style, but fully gray. He invited me to sit down in a fabric chair, the kind that sits in living rooms as he sat behind his large wooden desk. I found his office to resemble a room rather than an office. There was a comfy couch and a studio, where he broadcasts his daily show, which would occur 30 minutes after the completion of our interview.

I introduced myself and he immediately began to talk to me as if he had known me and like he had done interviews all his life. Very relaxed, poised, and engaged. From the start, I knew this interview would be interesting as I knew I would be interviewing an 84 year old man before my arrival, but the energy and tone of his voice felt like I was talking with an active 50 year old man. After telling me that he was going to dedicate a song to me and my mother (the person who suggested him for the interview) on his radio show, our interview began.

FAMILY BEGINNINGS

Well, I was born in the country, Telsa City. My mother and father ended up in Crown Point, that's on the river. We lived in Crown Point and I believe my career started at an early age of seven. Seeds, garden seeds. You could order garden seeds out of a catalog and they would send them to you and after you sold them, you could send them the money. And in some cases, I sold little bitties. You could order little bitty chickens for the house, for the home and we would do that too but I wouldn't sell the chickens, my mother would raise the chickens. But I would read the book, the almanac, and see where I could order seeds and I would sell also the Pittsburgh Courier, that was a Black newspaper printed in Pittsburgh, PA. That's how the Blacks got their news at that time. The Informer out of Darton was an old paper too but the Pittsburgh Courier was going into the little saw mill towns like Crown Point.

And I went to elementary school there and I think, looking back over my life, I think that's how and it will have to be something that's born within, I think that's how I got my career started in sales and business. And I used to parch peanuts and then sell the peanuts, like a nickel a bag, 10 cents a bag, something like that. I knew I did it, I knew I used to shine shoes but I can't remember how much I got for shining those shoes but I did shine shoes. It was like 10, 15 cent, 10 cents something like that; I would imagine that's what it was because at that time Coca-Cola was a nickel a bottle.

So my career started back in those days when I was a little boy and I guess that's something I had within. But anyway, I attended school there in Deville. They had a three room school house; you had elementary school, junior high, and high school all in the same building. Can you imagine that? And at that time teachers, if you didn't get your lesson, they'd whoop you with a switch and they would send you in the woods to get the switch. I'm going back to the beginning of my career. But I had enough sense to count my money which wasn't too much. So I think my career started at that time. But now jumping over to finishing high school in Redford; my father left Crown Point and moved to Redford. And he was working in Redford, so I had to go with him and my mother there. I think my mother and father separated in Crown Point, my daddy went to Redford, I went with him and my sister stayed with my mother.

In his autobiography, Richey recalled his father's parents being middle class owning farmland and livestock. His mother's parents were poor. He compared his grandparents and seems to favor his father's side and mentions his paternal grandmother was a great cook and paternal grandfather a hard worker. He stated his maternal grandmother was not a good cook and did not mention his maternal grandfather. Richey also recalled enjoying his visits to his paternal grandparents' home because he was able to ride horses, eat, watch cattle dip, work in the fields, and socialize with relatives. He mentioned as a child, he always thought big and desired to live in a big city.

In his book, Richey talked vividly about the fourth Sunday in August in Telsa City at the local church where people gathered for a big dinner.

They wore fancy clothes and rode in on their horses and wagons. In describing his childhood and family beginnings, he always seemed to make comparisons between rich and poor people, an economical divide. He also started working at the saw mill with his dad at the age of nine; it's important to remember at that time in America, this was common as there were no child labor laws and children were expected to help out with the family income.

EXISTENCE OF CAREER INFLUENCES AND ROLE MODELS

In his autobiography, Richey Donovan recounted Mr. Paisley, who owned houses, a lumber company, and a store in Crown Point, the town he grew up in. Richey referred to Mr. Paisley as a man who "called the shots" and was "king of the hill" because he printed his own money coupons for employees to shop at the store. Richey's admiration of Mr. Paisley was so strong that he thought the town should be named after him. In his book, he narrates "looking back, I realize now that he [Mr. Paisley] was one smart businessman. He controlled the town and everyone in it, including my father, who went to work at the Paisley Lumber Company shortly after we moved there from Telsa City."

Richey specified admiration for quality people of high standards. This seemed to include people who were businessmen, caring, and entrepreneurial. For example, he spoke of Mr. Sabe as the owner of Redford, who he admired once he moved with his dad after the split of his parents. He also mentioned how he admired his stay-at-home mother as well because she cooked for everyone and was a strong and fair person, characteristics he sought to duplicate. In a 1987 article featured in his book, it proclaimed Richey inherited sternness and sense of humor from his mother; Christianity and obedience from both parents; and thriftiness and real estate acquisition from his father.

No, nobody I wanted to be like, not even my daddy. I used to admire my grandfather. My grandfather, I don't know how that man came about all the property he had, because I didn't know his history. When I came up he was already doing good. My grandfather had a lot of land in Telsa City and he had a lot of cattle and horses and farmland. And when he died, he had split it up for all his children. He had about five or six and he had surveyed it all out to them. He's just that smart, he's the one that I admire my grandpa. And I guess I must have took something from him cause he had a lot of property.

In his book, Richey spoke highly of his father's side of the family and their career choices and career expectations for him. Richey mentioned his father had high expectations for him to be a doctor; but realized he did not have the proper foundational education to become one. Though he felt no pressure, he mentioned his father's side of the family were all college graduates and were doing well and they helped him. His uncle Zeff took him to his first professional football game and allowed him to use his truck to drive to his job at the Post Office. His uncle Prentice owned a bails bondsmen in Seattle. His aunt Evelyn allowed him to live with her when he went to live in Los Angeles to work at the Post Office.

MAKING MEANING OF CAREER EXPERIENCES

When I got to the University, my daddy sent me off to be a doctor. He wanted to see me be a doctor but when I got in college, I realized I didn't have the background from a segregated school in Redford to be a doctor. I didn't get much biology and chemistry and that was one of the requirements of entering med school. I had basic math and I was always good at math but biology and chemistry, I knew very little about solving those chemistry equations. We didn't know nothing about no biology, we were reading that out of a book. This is one of the results of segregated schools. We didn't have the same types of teachers. Our teachers weren't capable of what they were supposed to be teaching us. We got a lot of geography, we got a lot of math and I realized that when I got to the University, so I majored in tailoring.

I started there; I used to run a tailoring shop. I was cleaning clothes and making money cleaning clothes. I was waiting tables in the teachers' lounge in the cafeteria. See at the University at that time they had a cafeteria you get in line just like [a restaurant buffet line] and I was waiting on teachers. And I would take some of that meat home to the dormitory and on Sunday nights I would sell hamburgers and ham sandwiches with the meat I had stolen from the cafeteria. I guess I was a businessman from the get go. And I ran the cleaners and I would clean the president's, President Colin Peterson was the president of the University. He was the son of the original president William Rishon and I was cleaning his clothes, his suits, pressing suits. Most of his suits he just have them pressed because he didn't wear them much. He had so many of them. I would press his suits and I was making money pressing other people's clothes running the cleaners. And I don't know if anybody else could bring stuff, yeah they brought it in there and I was charging them. And I made money doing that.

In the meantime, my daddy was sending me money. We didn't have student loans at that time, I don't think so, I never did get one. But I stayed there taking the courses I need to take and after I finished I knew how to make clothes, I knew how to sew. I could take a piece of cloth, cut it out and lay it on the table and cut out a man's coat and pants. Just draw it out with measurement and everything, no pattern. Eventually I bought some patterns for a man's coat but before that I was drawing it out on the cloth with white chalk. And I went in business in Redford selling suits. Finally, I was doing so good that I could tell at that time I could bring my cloth over to Darton to the suit maker and they were making them wholesale. So I'd pay wholesale and then sell it retail. So I did that for a couple of years and if the weather got bad in Redford, most of the work was construction work and the construction workers couldn't get any jobs and they couldn't buy no clothes, so I left Redford and came to Darton.

And when I came to Darton, I had started a new thing. I came to Darton and worked at [the local furniture company], delivering furniture and eventually I started working at the Post Office. Living in Darton, I stayed here awhile then I moved to Los Angeles. The whole while I was here, I was waiting tables, doing different odd jobs, and went to Los Angeles and stayed there awhile working in the post office and then I went into the army.

I went into the army there and stayed in the army about three years. And when I got out the army I had to get in the reserve and staying in the reserve about three years and then I ended up back here in Darton. And I ended up in the post office and finally I went into business. Well let's see, while I was working at the post office, I'm trying to recall now. And being my age, you can't think of what you did yesterday.

While I was working at the post office, I think it was, they started a DJ school, a disc jockey school. Well I always knew my voice was different. If you listen to this tape you're gonna say this man sound different from any other man I ever interviewed. I always knew it was different and so I went to this DJ school and I went to the class and it was about 25 people in the class. I said 'you don't have that many black radio stations for all of us to get a job'. But I said 'if anybody get one, I'm going to get one'. So the guy called me after we finished, took about a year after I finished. They had an opening over at WZUP a friend of mine named James Freeman, I never will forget, he called and told me, said 'Richey Donovan they need somebody down at WZUP for a weekend'. And I went down there and the man gave me the job. Because the guy that had the school, they knew I was sounding different, I was different. So I worked there for about three years WZUP. Worked at WZUP on weekends, I would just open up on Sunday morning and I would stay there all day Sunday night til 12 Sunday night. Six o'clock Sunday morning til 12 Sunday night. I'd take a break for one hour for lunch and I stuck with that for about three years.

In the meantime while I was doing that week guest and weekend, the regular DJs, the drive times, AJ, her name was AJ, her name was Alma Jean, but her radio name was AJ. And so I would do her show four hours for $5. A whole four hours of radio disc jockey for $5. One name Scout, I did the whole show for him, you can get Richey Donovan to work anyplace. I was R. Donovan Jones then, whole four hours for $5. Then an opening came up for an evening DJ I think it was Sunday, Sunday evenings. Cause he would relieve me on Sunday evenings I had one splitting it. His name was Richey Rich and someway he lost his job and they gave it to me. And I became Richey Don. So what Richey Rich would do, AJ for 4 hours, $5, Scout four hours for $5, then they want to get off they were the main DJs at WZUP at that time. So I took that, I was doing that, I was getting that training.

Sometimes you have to intern, you got to do training. Nowadays you got to pay interns. Well they were paying me, $5 for four hours, alright. So an opening came up at WKRP, they heard me. They used to listen to me, they know how I sounded. So WKRP called me to come over there. When I got the evening drive, that's from 2p to sign off, that station was a sun up to sun down. They would call it a daytime station. A day time AM radio station is sun up to sun down. Sun up comes sometimes like the time changes, the station sign on 6am sometime, on 5am sometime 7am, sun up to sun down. Sometime I used to sign off at 5:30 and the sun would set in January, February sun sets about 5:30, okay I signoff and get into traffic. But it wasn't no traffic like it is now. There weren't many cars like it is now. We talking about the 50's, late 50's early 60's. That's what we talking about now. And I started working, but now when I started at WZUP that was 1957. That's when I started in radio.

In 19 and 57 and now its 2013 and I'm still in radio, I ain't making no progress. I'm just in a rut. (laughs) But I stayed there, I stayed working at that station. And while working at that station, I saved enough money to buy some *property on Avenue F. Real estate, I bought 2 ½ acres, 2 ¾ acres of land on Avenue F. Avenue F was a two lane road, two lane straight road in Cottonwood. I bought that property and I bought two lots out there. I was married to a school teacher at that time, she was saving her money, I was saving mine. And we bought a house she say "we got to buy a house first" I said "I want a business" but we got to buy a house first. Now I didn't know that I wanted a motel. You know what made me want a motel? At that time, I built a motel with the contractor for $32,000. Thirty-two thousand dollars back in '59, I opened it in '59. And the title company, the man that was at the title company, he said "Richey Donovan it's going to take you a long time to pay off this $32,000". You know he didn't think I could do it. He didn't know nothing about the motel business. I finished that motel, what nothing but 13 rooms, 13 room motel. When I finished that motel, and turned on the lights, boom here come a customer! "Ya'll open for business?" Yeah, shoot, I kept filling up, fillin up, fillin up, I used to do some business there.*

I grew to, when I left, when I gave it up, sold it, I had 123 rooms because at the same time on the same property I built some apartments, duplexes and I found the people hard to pay rent. It's hard to get your rent and they know the process of getting them out. So I took the duplexes and made them motel rooms. Water beds came into then, I made all of them waterbed row. I put waterbeds in all of them. Some of them I made two, four motel rooms out of a duplex. Four motel rooms out of one duplex! Then I built some more. I built one building, it's a picture of it out there, 40 rooms. First I started with 13, then I built one 26 I think it was, then the next building it was 40 and then I took the six duplexes that I had and made them motel rooms so the whole complex on the two and a half acres, I filled up the whole 2 ½ acres. I just kept investing, investing, investing.

Oh now listen to this, when I was working at the motel, running the motel, working as a DJ, I saw a recording artist. See we didn't have television and we didn't have FM radio. I had the city in the palm of my hands because I was good. And I'm still good at 85. Not as good as I used to be but I'm as good once as I was once. And once is good enough anyway. Can I get an amen?

The motel, I ran that place from 1959 to 1980 something. I got tired of doing it. I was making money. I was making big money. And then I recorded a group. You see that in my bio. And we lucked up with a record called "Tighten Up". Got to be a million selling record. The good Lord been blessing me all of my life. For the things that I've done and the places I've been. We got that "Tighten Up" record and from then on, my career just kept going up and up and up. And I kept investing and investing and investing. And we bought the radio station I was working for, five of us bought WKRP radio 1429.

And I was one of the owners but I got...and I ran for County Commissioner in 1976 and I found out how dirty politics is. That's a dirty game. Whooo that's dirty. So I said, I don't never want to get into politics anymore. I didn't know it was dirty. I don't backbite nobody! Back stabbing. You talk about backstabbing, it was guys coming to my meetings, finding out what I had going on, and going to my opponents meetings and telling them what Richey Donovan is doing. So I said I didn't want to do that anymore, so in the meantime, I had spent so much of my personal money, that I said I got to get my money back. So I went off the air, in order to run I had to get off the air. I could've gone back.

I don't know, it was just another thing to do. It's just another thing, you see, you take like the man Mitt Romney ran for president. What was his motivation? Just something else to do. He's rich, I had money. You don't know what to spend it on. You see these guys getting all this money get to dope. They don't know what to do with the money. I was almost in the same fix. Managing money is a course within itself. And so many of the athletes they get all the millions of dollars they don't know what to do with it. They start buying cars, and one time I had a truck, three Mercedes and a whole bunch of other cars and it took me a long time to realize why do I have all these cars? I can't drive but one. I had to buy battery charges to keep the batteries up in them. You know and it doesn't make any sense but I didn't realize it then. When you are young, you don't know what to do.

I talked with a guy that finished at the University and got a big bonus for signing with one of the professional teams. And I was talking to him and he said "Richey Don, I wished I had met you long time ago before I blew all my money". You know money managing is a course. You get a degree in that. And you have to love it. So I got mine from doing. I've been broke several times but I just have the ability to come back. And I always think big, I don't think about no ranky danky funeral home. You came up here, this is big!

You get me talking, you can't ask no question when I get to talking. Cause I done took you from a birth almost went back to this radio, I'm taking you to the funeral home. You now say 'how you get into the funeral business from entertainment?' And I'm going to show you a lot of pictures on the wall so you can add that to your thing. How you get from an entertaining radio DJ, I was playing rhythm and blues at WKRP. I knew about gospel from WZUP cause that's what I started on but today when I started with this station, it's been 15 years ago. I've been here in this building about 20 years. I was here about 5 years, maybe less when I went to KPPJ Gospel 1379. I knew about Gospel radio but when I was playing R&B, I'll say it again, you had no TV to promote your show. You had no DVDs, you had no FM radio. It was WKRP and everything was segregated. And a white station playing Johnny Taylor, they were calling that race music. But see I was playing Johnny Taylor, Bobbie Bluband, BB King, Temptations, Michael Jackson, all those people. We had the White people and Hispanic people that liked that music they were listening to us too. Different strokes for different folks. And they would listen to us and all those artist came to Darton.

Darton was a good promotional town; you could make a lot of money in this town. Always a lot of Black people here. James Brown, they all came to the radio station promoting their stuff. Michael Jackson, Lou Rawls, Muhammad Ali, he fought here. I M.C.'d a fashion show in between fights. The heavyweight, see when you have a heavyweight fight, they have about three preliminary fights, so in between the main event and the fight between them, I had a male fashion show and gave a prize to the winner. I have videos of this stuff. Everything I'm telling you and they roasted me just about at every club in town, including Corinthian Pointe. I have videos on all this stuff. They used to roast me.

I was looking at a roast the other day, my 65th birthday because I had just gotten my first check of social security, I retired and got my social security check at age 66. What did I retire from? I really, retired from the recording business. And I retired from the apartment business. And I sold the motel. I retired from the motel business. I had three motels and I didn't tell you about all the ones that I built. I built two on the north side, one on [the highway] and I never did go into it. I built it and sold it. I sold it before I built it. I had one with my uncle and we split up and I left him with that but we had two together.

But I never did like partners, I was in partnership with promoters and things and some of them would pay their part of the loss and I had to pay it all, so I'd rather be by myself. Even at the WKRP, me and the one of the owners, the manager, we didn't set horses to well. We got along but we finally went to court. (laughs) I'd just rather be by myself because I have different ideas and most of them don't think like I think. Even my wife don't think like I think. See when I went into this funeral business I was gonna have me four, just like I had motels, I had three or four. I built one over on the north side, I remodeled, I spent $30,000 remodeling a post office.

I was still the owner of WKRP, so I sold my interest out of there. Because I sold AM radio and I was looking at the ads of Johnson McCoy in the obituary they used to post things out there in the newspaper and read all them ads, I was like 'damn there must be some money in that business; so I bought this building and he [Todd] agreed to that. I said, "You want me to leave you a funeral home?" and he [Todd] said "yeah". And Jordan said his mother and father was dead. I said "you want to be my child?" He said "yeah". So Jordan came on in with us. But we were here about four-five years before Jordan came along. And then when Jordan came along it was the two of them and in the meantime, I started working on KPPJ, I was going down there to do an hour, and I was promoting this funeral home. And I still promote this funeral home. See I've been in advertising all my adult life almost, so I know the value of advertising so I kept on advertising Donovan & Sons, Donovan & Sons. And talking about Jones & Sons, Jones & Sons, Jones & Sons. And I still do.

PIVOTAL AND TURNING POINT EXPERIENCES IN CAREER

I had colon cancer and when I got well, see they thought I was going to die, I thought I was going to die. I was going to the health club and the guy said "Richey Don you better start [seeking retirement] at 62 cause you may not make it to see 65" but I'm 85.

Richey's stint in the motel business was also during segregation, when there were few hotels for Blacks to stay in Darton. He recalled "I went to one [motel] once and saw all those people going in there getting those hourly rates and I said 'damn, must be a lot of money in this business.' So I said, 'I want a motel," and this was the turning point that got him started in this business that he would do for many years. However, this business did not come with immediate support from his family and also led to another pivotal experience in his career.

He continued,

And my wife at that time said "I help you get the motel if we get a house first". So he [Todd] didn't want no motel and I'm a good man. But I have my vices (laughs) okay, so I said okay I'm going to leave something for my son. 'What you want?' He said 'I want to go to Mortuary College'. So he went to Mortuary College.

CONTINUANCE OF THE LEGACY

Well see, I have one son, Todd Jones. One adopted son, Jordan Daniels. Todd he went to the University and he didn't make no progress. I think they put him out or something. I had a recording studio and I thought he wanted to get into that and I could make it bigger and bigger and bigger. In the recording studio at that time when he came along, it was getting more high tech and I had an engineer in there and every month or two months, the engineer had seen something new come out. And that's the way it is right now, cell phones come out every three-four months. So it was in the recording business same way, a lot of stuff comes out. So the engineer said we need such and such thing and I'd go buy it. Then I said "hey man" and then my son he got in the place and didn't want to fool with it no more.

I said "wait, I got to find you, you got to find you a job". So I said, "What you want?" he said "I want to be an embalmer". "An embalmer, what's that?" He said "a funeral home, I want a funeral home". I said "you don't want the motel?" I had the motel then. And the recording studio was at the Venus Motel. And he said "no, I don't want no motel". He grew up there. He was raised at the motel. Okay. So he went to Mortuary College. I said 'I'll get you a funeral home', so I was going to make my house a funeral home because it's on a lot of property. My wife say "I'm not gonna live in no funeral home". So I saw this building for sale. I was just riding looking for property. This used to be a bank and I saw it for sale. I said "damn I can get that, I can get that building". So I went to who it was listed with and found out how much it was they told me and I put up a down payment.

I don't consider myself nothing but a human being. Legacy what is that to me? I don't know nothing about that. What is legacy? I don't know. To live right, do right, help other people and die and go to heaven if there is a heaven. I hope it is. I've been taught that there was but I never died and come back and don't know nobody else that died and came back. Me being in the death business, that's what I'm taught, that's what I read, that's what I believe.

SENSE OF BELONGING AND COMMUNITY

Though Richey does not believe in legacy, he is a strong believer in community. In a newspaper article as cited, "It was his ability to inspire young people to believe they could become successful in the music industry that made the real difference for him." He was known for his public appearance and engaging the community. "Richey Don's style would bring together an older, rural form of humor and recast it in a developing urban atmosphere". "It was his ability to inspire young people to believe they would become successful in the music industry that made the real difference for him".

Additionally, Richey used his talents and connections to help his pastor grow his church from 15 members to a mega-church in the United States. Additionally, he held several benefit concerts that were free to the community and were mainly done to unite the community.

He explained,

I took Mt. Zion Evangelist Temple, Faith Temple Baptist, a Methodist church and a Church in God in Christ, I put them together at Moon Center and I paid the bill and it was free to the public. If you talk to Bobbie Murray ask him about it. I had posters out on the streets; I had the three pastors from different denominations and three choirs from different denominations at Moon Center downtown.

Second Generation

Richey's career legacy became the foundation for the Jones family career legacy. Richey's sense of community translated to the attitudes and behaviors of his sons. Additionally, in his generative thinking, his desire to leave Todd something, resulted in a continuation of his legacy through the evolution of his career. The purchase of the Jones & Sons Funeral Home added a facet to his legendary career that his sons now have a role.

After my interview with Richey and guided tour of the wall of fame that precedes his upstairs office, I went downstairs to interview his two sons Todd and Jordan together. At a conference table in Todd's basically decorated office, Todd and Jordan seemed very timid and unsure of the interview. But after a brief introduction and quick overview of my intentions, the two seemed to relax and our interview began.

What is interesting is they do not have an extensive career story because their careers where perceived as a calling and they knew early on what they wanted to do and through support of family and friends, they set out to do it and continued to enjoy their careers, which they feel gives glory to God. Their answers were similar and piggy-backed off of each other; therefore, their interviews were incorporated into the categories together and signified by their names for their individual responses and comments.

FAMILY BEGINNINGS

Todd responded,

I wanted to go into the funeral business cause as a child I was always interested. My mother she's from South Louisiana and when we would go to South Louisiana, there was a particular funeral home in New Iberia, Louisiana. A big building and they used to have a lot of ambulances and hearses outside and I was always interested and I never knew what that was and that started the interest of the funeral business and that's what I had always wanted to be.

Jordan added,

And so as a kid growing up I played the minister, the dead person, and the undertaker, what they called us at that time. I had no idea that this would be one of my dreams. And so I've been doing this ever since I was 16 years old.

EXISTENCE OF CAREER INFLUENCES AND ROLE MODELS

Todd shared his thoughts of the influential people that affected his career.

Well mine was like different entertainers, beside my father he was a big role model, and a lot of entertainers that he introduced me to such as James Brown, George Clinton. And then you had people here in Darton, Jesse Anderson, Chuck Clay, a lot of people, entertainment moguls, David Miles and then a lot of ministers that have gone on, which was a cousin of my father's was Barron White and then a lot of the old funeral directors. Mr. Kevin Johnson had a big funeral home in Wilshire. Those would be my role models. There were more strong leaders. They were people that you didn't hear any negativity about such as what you hear today. You know the ministers they were higher echelon people and people looked to them for guidance even a lot of the entertainers you didn't hear anything negative about drugs or anything. They even gave back to the community; did benefits, would come here to Darton to do benefits. My dad would ask them for different things say 'I need you to do a benefit for this'. "Well Richey, no problem" you know just positive influences.

Jordan commented,
Yeah bout the same. They were positive people in the community. They did positive things in the community to help people. They were not the type of people that were out there trying to rob, steal, or kill. So when you see someone that is positive in the community that was well educated, they gave back to the community.

SUPPORT
Todd remembered how his parents set career expectations for him; ironically, the same expectations Richey's father had for him.
They [my parents] tried, wanted me to be a physician and I didn't want to be. Either a radio announcer or a physician and I didn't want to do that so, I ended up doing something else but it came back to this full circle.

They did not speak about support but tremendous support existed because Richey Don spoke about how, because of the career aspirations of Todd, he bought the funeral home for him, despite his desire to have Todd follow in his footsteps. In addition, Jordan stated he received support through friends. His parents died, and then by Richey taking him in as his son and creating space for him to live out his career in the family business are demonstrative of support for his career choice.

FAMILY VALUES
Jordan stated "responsibility". However, Todd provided more detail.
And honesty. Being or having a word. That's a main object as of now a day. People don't have words. Used to be back when I was a kid, your word was your bond. If you asked me to do something and I told you I could do it, you looked toward me as holding that word. Nowadays when you ask someone to do something they'll say "uh yeah I can do it". Then when you go over there for them to do it, "ah man" everybody comes up with excuses. Today's generation is full of excuses. When I was a kid, no such thing as excuses. My dad said "take can't out of your vocabulary, you can do it". He say "the only thing that stop you from doing something is yourself". You stop yourself!

SENSE OF BELONGING AND COMMUNITY
Jordan replied,
And so I made myself a promise, in fact a couple of years ago, every summer I used to by paper and pencils and everything to give to the kids and so I made myself a promise that when God blesses me I want to be a blessing to others. As they gave back, we're in a position now that God has blessed us that we give back.

(Todd)
But you can't pat yourself on the back and say I did it, you better say "thank you" to Him. That's it and then when you have a staff of folks that are working with you and cause this is a team. It ain't no little I's or big I's we all in this together. If I mess up, we all mess up. If he mess up, we all mess up. We gotta make everybody look good for the boss up there, my daddy, Richey Don, ain't that right Jordan? Cause he'll tell you in a minute "cause people gone call me and say 'Richey Don, them boys messed up over there". And he tell us all the time, "Ya'll don't know it, I'll be out and people be telling me your boys they took care of business, they treated me nice, and they didn't take all my money either".

MAKING MEANING OF CAREER EXPERIENCES
(Todd)
Helping someone in their time of need because that is what the main goal is. In death that is a critical time in a person's life. It is not an everyday occurrence. When it happens, you don't know the individual. It's almost like you hear the old cliché "I know how you feel" no you don't know how a person feel. Because every individual takes in different and we would like to be remembered as individual persons that helped the clients that came through our doors of being some type of influence that made a difference in that transitional period. That's what I would like to be remembered as.

I worked for the City of Darton then I worked for my father when he had another business, but in the neighborhood it was a funeral home and I got to be friends with one of the owner's sons. And then he came into it, you know when his daddy became ill, and then he would let me hang around and I would see things and then that's how I really got a little bit more in to it.

(Jordan)

Well I got into the funeral business, my fraternity brother's family owned a funeral home in Louisiana. And out of all the other jobs I ever had I'd say that this is the job that I liked the most, enjoy doing because I'm serving families. From the time I was in high school, I worked every summer at elementary schools but as far as the funeral business, no. There's two songs that put me in the mind when you asked that question. "May the work that I have done speak for me", that's one of the songs. And there's another Black history song that puts me in the mind that if I can help somebody and that I can cheer somebody with a song that my living shall not be in vain.

...My passion is to make sure that my family doesn't have to struggle, that's one of my main passions and concerns and to make sure that the families that we serve here, when they leave this place they left feeling somewhat satisfied and pleased with our services. Because when it comes to the families that we serve, we take it personal as though if it were our own. And so wherever we go, if we should have a death in the family in another state we feel as though they should treat our families as well as we treat others. That's my main passion especially in this business. If my families are happily satisfied, then I am.

It's here where you get to see how the spirituality comes into play with their career decisions. Todd and Jordan begin to reference their career as a passion and spiritual calling. This calling holds them to a moral standard in how they perform and thus their career carries into their personal lives as well. This is an example of their career identity, where they begin to describe or identify themselves based on their career and the characteristics of what it means to be successful at said career. Same as their father identifies himself as a businessman, which is synonymous to his career and how he conducts himself in and out of business. The ability to accept your career as a calling is taking the step into leaving your legacy.

(Todd)

You only get one shot to do it right. You can't make mistakes, mistakes are costly. And so you have to want to be the best that I can be and you know and you can't half step and when they walk through the door I should be on point to be able to help them. That's what the main passion is. Like they told us at school, you should want to do this with a passion even if you couldn't get paid for it. You know just like a minister, you have some ministers that say 'I don't do it for the compensation, I do it for the glory of God'. This is actually a ministry. This is our calling. God gave all of us talents. He gave you a talent, gave me a talent, gave my brother a talent. Our talent is to help someone. That's why we're here. We're not supposed to just sit here and like a bump on a log. When people come through the door they looking for help. And they asking for help and guidance and that's what we try to provide help and guidance.

Help them transition from point A to point B and we continue to still help because we also tell them that the service doesn't stop after we come from the cemetery. Our passion also is that people still call us for guidance continually for things that they don't know or understand. You have to step out the box. Sit in the seat with the person, don't just sit across from them you know and 'yes ma'am and yes sir'. Put yourself in that situation. Move yourself from here and sit here vice versa and then you'll understand. Yes ma'am.

Families saying the job well done, when we walk them in that chapel. And you know they have the confused look on their face, they not ready to go in but when they go in and they look at their loved one and then they look up at you and say "I didn't think you could do it but ya'll did it." And the thing that we tell them "it wasn't us, it was Him". That's the main joy. That supersedes it. When that family, whether they paid you $10 mil or $1, you should treat the same way. Cause if you treat them any kind of way, they will pick that up. They will say "they treated me, I guess it was cause of the money I spent they treated me like that". You want to make them...like a friend of mine used to say "roll that red carpet out" and sometimes they never have gotten the red carpet, they say everybody that come to your door should get that red carpet treatment from the beginning when they walk into the door until the end. And then they say "I know where I want to go when I leave this world, Jones & Sons Funeral Home over there with Todd and Jordan and Richey Don. Or better yet, is this Richey Don's place? (laughs) That's where I wanna go, Richey Don's place!"

I'm going to add to that. When you in the grocery store shopping and folk come up to you and smile and say "hey man you buried my mother, you buried my father" and a little kid walk up to you and they say "yeah you buried my grandmother" you be in the cleaners and folks know you and walk up to you "hey baby how you doing?" You be in a restaurant, you sittin down eating, people come up to you "hey how ya'll doing? You know man ya'll sure did, man, ya'll surely put so and so away" you know that makes your day verses you sit there and folks see you and they look at you and you know their family looking at you and they go the opposite direction, which, thank God, we ain't never had that happen, knock on wood. But when they come up to you and pat you on the back or even if you're at another funeral and they see you and they say "you may not remember me but you buried so and so and you didn't know this my cousin ya'll got and I told them to come to you all cause ya'll treated us nice". You know and "make sure ya'll come back to the church and eat dinner with us and feed them boys, feed them first before you feed everybody else".

So and little things, a lot of times people come by and drop off gift cards and say "man hey, I don't have any money but won't you and your brother go out to eat" and you say man, you was planning on going to a fast food restaurant, we can go to an actual sit-down restaurant. Things like that you don't be looking for but you did something and you made somebody's day and you made somebody's night get better. And they tell you and even if people call you on the phone at 8p, 9p, 10p or 11, 12 at night you sleep and you get up it makes a difference when you wake up and they say" I'm sorry I'm disturbing you, I don't know what to do". And you say "what's going on?" And they say somebody has passed. Or they pay, ask you for a price list sometimes you be wanting to tell them "baby this ain't a time to talk about price" and then you catch it before you even say it you go on and tell them and they tell you "well you know what, okay thank you". Then you get a call the next day and they say "you know what, I called a bunch other funeral homes but you talked to me and it was two in the morning and you made me so at ease and I told the rest of the family when she make that transition, call on over there to Jones & Sons" that's when you know you doing something right and you know you can pat yourself on the back and you also tell them thank you.

(Jordan)

The main focus is loyalty and it puts me in the mind of the quote that Gladstone wrote that I have at my home, and it says about loyalty and it talks about respect. And when you in this business, loyalty means a lot and respect means a lot. So that's the most important thing when it comes to the families, they're looking for respect, they're looking for honesty, they're looking for loyalty. Like he said "show me the manner in which a nation or community cares for its dead and I will measure with exact mathmaticalness [sic] the respect for the law of the land and their loyalty to high ideals", so when whatever you do be good at it and be loyal. And once you bless others, the blessing will come back to you.

(Todd)

Amen. I can't speak for everybody but here doing positive things, serving families, we up all hours of the night, the phone never stops ringing, we have to answer. I answer that phone 365 days a year, seven days a week. You be trying to take a shower. I have the cell phone right there. I had to cut the shower off, rush over there and then I say "excuse me I was taking a shower but hold on let me dry myself off". Because they want you, something happened and because if you can't do it, someone else will. They'll tell you in a minute, if you can't do it, someone else will. So you have to be information. They call us for information, they call me, they call him for information, because they feel comfortable with us for anything. They walk in the door and they don't know and you can't be mean to our senior citizens because they uneducated. You can't look down upon them because they expect you to do that cause they figure you got an education but you have to kind of check yourself, then get on their level.

CONTINUANCE OF THE LEGACY

(Todd)

Definitely we would want that [for our children to be involved in the business]. You know but like he said, it's up to them you know it's up to them but we hope and pray that they would carry it on because that's what we building a foundation of this, you know we would be considered the first generation funeral directors. My dad is not, he just the owner. So me and Jordan, we are the first generation and we looking for that second generation and then the legacy we don't want it to just stop with us and then die out. We want to be a force to be reckoned with and continue forever.

(Jordan)

That is the goal. But you can bring your children in the world and give them the best education in the world but it's up to them, it's their choice. Would we love it? To carry the name on? Of course. Our kids are small, so if they not in school then every once in a while we will bring by the funeral home and let them get acclimated and show them around and things of that nature. Let them have a little hands on experience, not too much (laughs) but we'll let them have a little hands on experience and if they have questions, we're here to answer it. My daughter, she's more interested than my son. She's very inquisitive.

Todd concluded with his definition of legacy and what it means to his family career legacy. "Growth, and continuation you know, never ending. It's like God left a legacy, his people are still continuing on from Adam and Eve till the present and it's going to continue on".

Chapter Summary

The Jones family career legacy is different from others because the career path is not in the same exact footsteps. However, their commitment, values, and goals are the same and all together, the trio is working in the family business to preserve a legacy centered on community. What is special about their legacy, is it demonstrates younger generations can influence the career decisions of older generations. It provides a different outlook on the familial influence and how legacies can be created and maintained. Todd and Jordan were able to fulfill their calling on the basis of Richey Don's personal career legacy, which has merged the careers of two generations and has begun to set the tone for the next generation in the funeral home business.

Here are the lessons learned about family career legacy from the Jones family in a nutshell.

1. Find purpose in your career
   a. Seek a career that is fulfilling and gives you a purpose
   b. Accept what you have been called to do by assessing your strengths, weaknesses, desires, and dreams
   c. Be in-tune with your spiritual and/or moral compass
2. Build a support network
   a. Find a mentor who can guide you in your career and who has achieved the things you would like to accomplish
   b. Surround yourself with people who will support you and your dreams
3. Become community-oriented
   a. Begin to think about how you can help others who are less-fortunate
   b. Think of ways you can improve your community and/or the situations that suppress others

    c. Work for a greater cause than yourself
4. Think generatively
    a. Think about how you want to be remembered
    b. Establish things and ways you will be remembered
    c. Think about how you can improve the lives of your children
    and what you can do to provide them with a leverage for their
    careers
5. Be open to expand your legacy and not be limited to just one
job or one particular industry

CHAPTER 6

"The greatest legacy one can pass on to one's children and grandchildren is not the money or other material things accumulated in one's life, but rather a legacy of character and faith." --Billy Graham

Having a legacy is filled with so many components but the pulse of each legacy is the character transmitted through generations and the faith in the form of provision for the future. The values and belief systems of families become the cornerstone of the family reputation and their identity of how they are to behave, perform; ergo, what it means to be a member of that family. Proverbs 22:1, tells us that "a good family name is rather to be chosen than great riches", stressing the importance of displaying good character over the emphasis of financial success. Sure, each career legacy would like to provide a living for their families and see it continue throughout generations, but the financial security will come when the good moral character is upheld.

It is evitable that with every success comes failure, but a resilient character base will always rise to the top, despite the external pitfalls and barriers. It's synonymous with the old adage, 'you give someone a fish they eat for a day, but if you teach them how to fish, they eat for a lifetime'. Money and material things depreciate and are temporary but knowing how to obtain such things, are permanent because they are embedded in who a person is and that is passed on to those they influence. Essentially, legacies are patterns teaching future generations of family and community members to not only exist but to be impactful in leaving the world a better place.

The last family in this book I will introduce you to is the Callagari family. They are a God-fearing family who have achieved financial and social success through generations of family business. However, their maintenance of business ethics, rooted in family values of hard-work and honesty and a heart for the community have guided their accolades and established a legacy to be remembered in the lives of young people for generations to come.

The Callagari Family: Legacy of Martial Arts

This family career legacy consists of a blended family who own and operate a martial arts business in the suburbs of a major metropolitan city in the southern United States. Full Force is a martial arts school that teaches TaeKwonDo, Krav Maga, and self-defense classes to children beginning at the age of four to adults of all ages. Additionally, the goal of the school is to not only teach fighting techniques but life lessons, discipline, confidence, physical fitness, and respect for all persons.

A Christian-based family, the Callagaris, run this family oriented business environment. Clinton is the founder and owner of Full Force and serves as the chief-instructor of the school. He is a 5th Dan AAU TaeKwonDo certified black belt and international referee who runs the school with his wife Thelma, a 2nd Dan TaeKwonDo Black Belt and a level three Krav Maga instructor. Clinton's son, Tobias a 3rd Dan TaeKwonDo Black Belt, serves as an instructor at the school, along with his daughter who teaches on an adhoc basis, who is a 5th Dan AAU TaeKwonDo certified Black Belt. Thelma's son Omar is the newest addition to the family business; he works at the front reception area on the administrative side.

This legacy is told from the points of view of Clinton, Thelma, Tobias, and Omar. Clinton and Thelma have no biological children

110

together, but each have children from a previous marriage. All of Clinton's children are adults and Thelma has three teen-agers that live in the same home as she and Clinton. Their interview takes place individually at the school. Clinton was interviewed in his secluded upstairs office, while the other three interviews were conducted in Thelma's downstairs office, near the front reception area. Their family career tree (Figure 6) includes all the other members of the family, including those who are a part of the business that were not interviewed.

About Full Force

Honored by a major private university as one of best small businesses for its responsiveness to its community, Full Force Martial Arts (Full Force) has received awards in the vein of Family Business of the Year, Stewardship Award, and Small Family Business Award, to name a few. You would not know the many accolades of this family business by talking to any of the family members but you would feel their accomplishments immediately entering the school.

Opening the door, the cool air-conditioning greets its visitors as you enter directly into the front reception area. Behind a big, basic wooden desk about six feet from the door sits Omar, who provides a warm welcome. To the right, the wall is decorated with multiple plaques documenting the family's many accolades. What immediately catches the eye is a large frame and picture of the family in a magazine article from 2011. To the left is a shelf of various forms of martial arts paraphernalia and directly in front of the entrance door is a framed United States flag that was flown from Iraq in honor of Clinton. Under the flag, was a poster of an attractive brunette (who I later found out is another one of Clinton's daughters) advertising nutritionist services. Immediately to the right, the front reception area opens to a view of the gym with bleachers located on the outside of the glass of the closed-in gym and a long hallway.

After waiting for a few minutes, I was greeted by Thelma who took me down the long hallway that passed her typical office of a mahogany desk with a computer and stacks of paper covering it, complete with a printer behind the desk, and along the wall a file cabinet. Then I was introduced to Clinton who took me to the end of the hallway, up the stairs, around the corner to the first and only office on the second floor that overlooked the massive gym. In his office, remnants of unique items, possibly collected from different parts of the world filled his office. From a traditional cuckoo clock, to life sized, hand carved art, swords, to framed pictures and everything else in between. Walking in his office, I felt like I entered into a "man cave" that was a visual collage of the many stories and experiences of Clinton's world. Upon entering, he immediately offered me a seat in a tall burgundy chair in front of his desk, as he assumed a seat behind his large, wooden desk that was covered with many stacks of paper. I sat down and our interview began.

Pursuing Legacy

Figure 6: The Callagari Family Career Tree

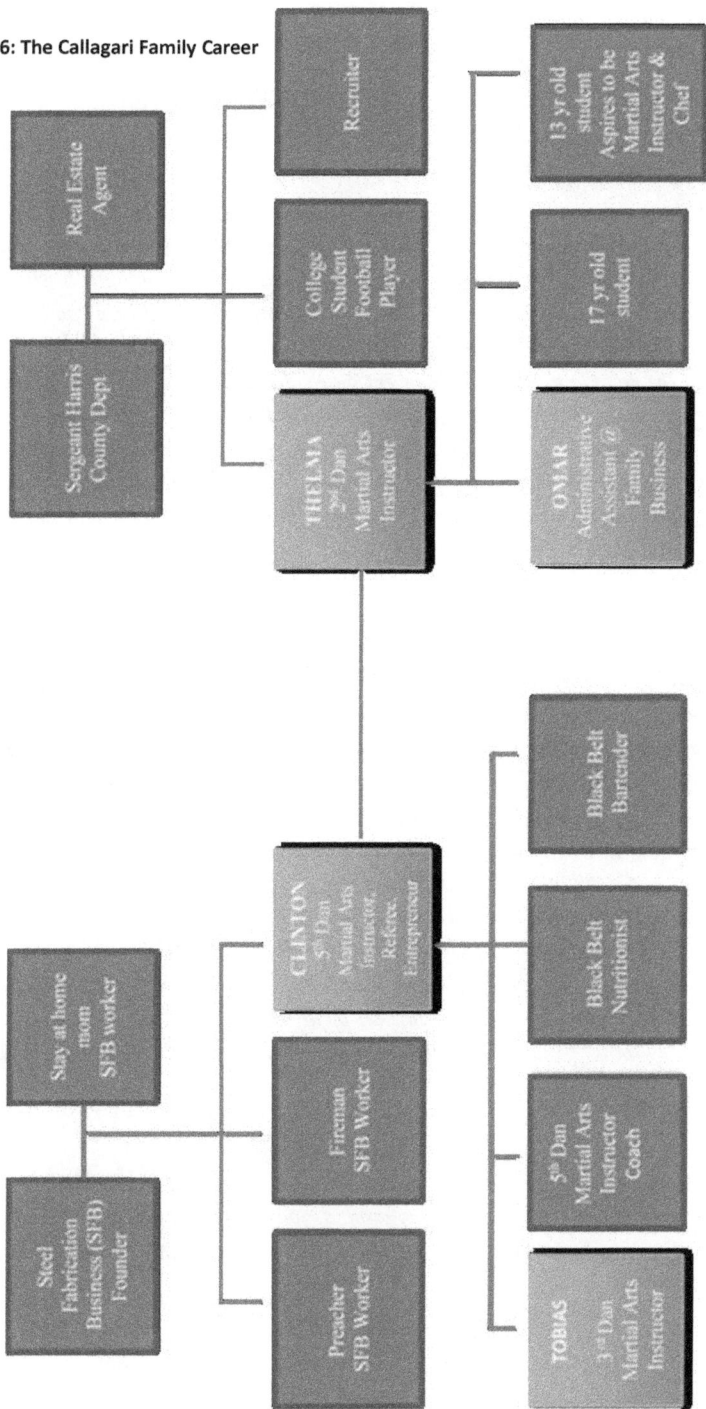

CLINTON'S STORY

FAMILY BEGINNINGS

My earliest career ambition when I was a kid? Would have been a veterinarian, probably around the age of 10 or 11. Well, my family we had…and we still have a steel fabricating business and we started when we were like 12 years old or so. And even before then my father was in the steel business, he would bring stuff home for us to do when I was like 5, 6, 7 years old putting bolts and nuts together. Well let's see when I was like 5, 6, 7, 8 years old my dad would bring home nuts and bolts from the steel fabricated business for us to sit in the garage and thread the nuts onto the bolts to make sure they went on good so there wouldn't be problems when they got onto the field. We would do that for money and everything. I know I worked in the rice fields for a summer or two, you know driving the hopper wagons and shoveling the rice. So it's just, you know, it wasn't any, you know, you just did it. Then when we were 12 we started our own business; well my dad did and gave each of us kids ownership in it.

EXISTENCE OF CAREER INFLUENCES AND ROLE MODELS

Well, he [my dad] started when he was 19 years old in the steel fabricated business and worked his way up. He was sweeping floors all the way to knowing how to do everything in the business. And today he is undisputedly the best in the business in the world and people acknowledge that. Actually, he's a quiet guy, he doesn't say much, he thinks about things a lot and awhile and does them and everything in the right way, the best possible way to do it. I learned my business ethics and everything and beliefs from him. Just you know, work ethic, hard work ethic, work more hours and honest, and to be honest in everything we do and to put out quality product. Honesty, quality, treating people fairly, taking care of your employees, treating them right and everything. That's very big with my dad. You know whenever times get bad instead of laying people off, he puts them to work cleaning things, fixing things, whatever till we pick up. You know he finds stuff for them to do.

PRESSURE

Like when I quit or tried to quit the steel fabricated business to do this full-time, my father wanted me to stay around, you know keep me around to help with the family business. So, you know, like 'you need insurance, you can still work a

114

couple days a week' and this and that, so try to keep me around and keep me in it. My dad is getting ready to be 85 years old and works every day and he still runs everything and he has made no plans on who's gonna run it when he goes away, when he passes, and he is not planning on retiring. He'll be there until...you know...he doesn't want to sell it. So, my oldest brother who is getting ready to be 65 is wanting to retire at the end of this year. I'm the only who has the business sense to run it, so we really don't have a clue what the hell is gonna happen.

I know for a fact that at the steel fabricating business that my three brothers and sister still work there full time; I'm just part-time. They used to feel pressure to have to be there a lot and I did because it was a family business and to put in extra work. I know one of them feels at least that no matter what they do, it isn't good enough. Um social pressure, financial, well that kind of stuff we don't really deal with that because we're all okay there.

I used to feel that they [my siblings] thought I wasn't working as much as I should at the steel fabricating business. I kind of felt like they thought I was being given stuff because I wasn't working there as much but to me they didn't understand how much time I was putting into this business, which was my passion.

SUPPORT

Well, the veterinarian I think his name was Dr. Hill, if I remember right, you know he kinda encouraged it some. Ah, no one in particular discouraged me, except the amount of school discouraged me. Uh, they [my parents] just let me decide on what I really wanted to do. If you wanted to do something they would support you. Just like when I decided to become an airline pilot, they supported me in that, helped me buy an airplane and get my time built. And when I left the business to go and work for the airlines, they supported that and helped me out there. My parents could afford to loan me the money and I'd ask them and I would pay them back with interest. You know it's easier than a bank. In fact they encouraged me to do so instead of going to a bank. They would support you in whatever you were doing, if it was the right thing to do. If it was Godly, otherwise, they wouldn't be behind that.

Clinton went on to describe his family values as lessons displayed by his father through business interactions saying "Honesty, quality, treating people fairly, taking care of your employees, treating them right and everything. That's very big with my dad".

PIVOTAL AND TURNING POINT EXPERIENCES IN CAREER

Well I drove trucks for a couple of years. I started working in the steel shop and then when I got married I moved inside and started doing the inspection and estimating and quoting and running the engineering department and purchasing and everything else as a young guy. And then I decided I liked flying, so I started flying and got hired on by Continental airlines and went and flew for them for several years. The business wasn't so good there and my upgrade status looked like I was gonna have to go to Guam. My father was getting older and me and my brother talked that he would probably retire soon and he and I would start running the business together. So I left the airlines and came back and my father never retired. I left, my brother left, he came back and you know and my father is still there.

I got into martial arts. Well I did TaeKwonDo when I was a kid, like 12, 13 years old but then about 17 years ago my daughter wanted to do martial arts or karate. So my wife found a place for her and she started class and a couple of other kids as well and they talked me into it and said 'dad, you used to do this. Why don't you come and take class with us?' or whatever so, I did and I started taking class and after we got our black belts, the owner of the school talked me into taking the school over. So I inherited one school, took over two more. We had about three schools and then my wife passed away and I was raising teenagers and working at the steel fabricating business. Work, teach, and running one school and the other two schools I was in charge of them too. So I finally told them guys they would have to buy them schools from me and run them themselves or I was shutting them down. So I combined to this one and this one exploded on me and became super big. So that's how I got into the martial arts business. In 2001 my wife died and a few months later we had 9/11; her dying kind of pushed me to do what I wanted to do in the martial arts field and everything more.

MAKING MEANING OF CAREER EXPERIENCES

Who was the most influential in creating my career identity? Wow, there's not one. Honestly. Um…I would have to go back to my dad again because I kind of run my business like he does. I learned my business ethics and everything and beliefs from him.

I've become an international referee, so I travel around the world refereeing TaeKwonDo championships. I'm leaving tomorrow to go to Russia to do the para TaeKwonDo, which is the special needs and it's gonna be the largest one ever they've ever had and it's gonna be the one that's hopefully gonna get them into the Paralympics in 2020 in Tokyo. So I'm leaving tomorrow to go referee there then I'll referee in Florida in a few weeks then I'll go to, in August, I go to Australia and Costa Rica. Two weeks ago I was in Austria, in Germany before that, Netherlands before that, Dominican Republic, Canada, you know, I go all over the world now to referee and gives me an excuse to travel and I love to travel. It costs money, I don't make any money doing it, but I enjoy it. I get to help a lot of people. You know we teach special needs, so that appeals to me. I got a heart for those guys.

CONTINUANCE OF THE LEGACY

My oldest daughter she's a fifth degree master instructor and I mean I've always encouraged her to do martial arts and she loves it and she does it. She went to college and got her degree and I got another...my other daughter she just graduated and she's a nutritionist and she's wanting to do some of her work out of here. So I encourage them to do whatever they want to do. My oldest son he works here, I wish he would take more ownership in it. I hear I probably try to put pressure on my son to be here more and put a little more effort into running and managing things and he just, um or my opinion doesn't do it and I got reasons why he doesn't and I'm not going to go into that. My younger son is the one I had to fire and he asked me the other day is there any possibility of him ever coming back to work here and I said "no, I don't think so" cause we can't get along.

My wife's youngest son, he's 13, he kinda wants to be a chef. So whenever we go down to our house in Cayman he goes to work for a local restaurant down there and a guy from Australia has a restaurant and he works for him, you know a few days a week at the restaurant seeing and learning what it is like to become a chef and everything. He just got his black belt a few weeks ago, well right about a month ago, yeah and he wants to become an instructor too, so we'll see.

I hope to leave...this martial arts school prosperous with them running it without me. You know and them to have learned good business practices and honesty and dealing with everybody and mainly doing whatever it takes to produce the best product possible and to help as many people as possible. That's what I really hope to achieve.

The meaning of success is enjoying what you're doing and being able to provide a living for your family and creating a legacy. I mean I'm trying to create a legacy and I think I'm doing it, so if you can create a legacy and leave something for your family but also so people will say, "I remember that guy started this", "I remember that guy did this", and "helped these people". That's a legacy that would be a success. Leaving a legacy and that's something you enjoy.

Clinton's desire to leave a legacy through his career and martial arts business is only part of his legacy. During the interview, he shared with me in detail his newest business venture in making a brand to be displayed on a multitude of things, starting with bamboo cups. Perhaps, his career as an entrepreneur is influenced more than he knows by the entrepreneurial spirit of his father. His father, who after starting his own business incorporated his children, who still have ownership and work there.   Clinton, ironically, after various explorations with other careers, has done the same with Full Force.

TOBIAS' STORY

Clinton's son, Tobias, was the only one of his biological children available for an interview and is employed full-time at the school. What I found interesting about Tobias was that he was the only one with an athletic build. He had a buzz cut hairstyle and came in very casual, wearing an old t-shirt and shorts with flip flops. He appeared to be in his late 20's and stood about 5'10. Late for the interview and from my observation, almost a bit tardy to prepare for his class. Regardless, Tobias sat down for the interview. In contrast to his step-brother Omar, his answers were frequently to the point. One statement Tobias made that summarized his personality and approach to his role at Full Force was,

I like to exercise, so being able to work out every day and run around with kids and stuff. Um I also enjoy just teaching and coaching being able to and the fact that I'm teaching and coaching about a subject that I really enjoy helps a lot. And I don't have to wear shoes.

In Thelma's office, Tobias gives his account of the family business and his career story.

FAMILY BEGINNINGS

I think I was probably, six or seven, or even before that, I think I wanted to play in the NFL. Football was my sport growing up, so I thought I was, everybody thinks they're going to be in the NFL. Lots of people encouraged me, my parents were probably my biggest support. They took me to my first football camp and drove me to practices and games and all that stuff. I don't think I really had anybody discouraging, you know telling me not to be the best you can.

I was already doing TaeKwonDo and we ended up buying a school and running it and I just kind of... one thing led to another. I still tell my dad "yes sir" and "no sir" and "yes ma'am, no ma'am". So I was always raised like that and I had a lot of friends that thought that was so weird that we would do that and that's just something, that's just how it was. My brother, I don't have any kids, but my brother and sister both have kids and their kids are taught to do that, and you know I think it's becoming even more rare now. I'm not religious but growin' up it was important and I think for most of my family it is still important.

EXISTENCE OF CAREER INFLUENCES AND ROLE MODELS

I just watched my grandfather, my parents, and my grandparents were really all hard workers. Whenever they decided they were going to do something, they put everything they had into it. So I think that had a big influence and obviously, we do martial arts and it was a lot of working out and doing the sport together.

Hmm, which one did I admire the most? I'd say either of my grandfathers. It's pretty hard to say which I admire the most. They both were good men, very loyal and self-made guys, very hard workers. Those were the qualities I admired the most, you know. I would say my dad since we're both here and both wanting to take this in the same direction.

I guess my dad had a pretty big influence on the shaping of my career identity. Working for him here, training with him, off and on I've been here. I've always had another job in between there but I always ended up back here, so my dad. The thing that we have always done and the thing we encouraged our students to do also is just to have respect for your elders when you talk to them. Hard work, I think that's a top one and loyalty to the family and for most of my family, their religion I think.

PRESSURE & SUPPORT

He [my dad] probably feels more pressure than I do and I probably feel more pressure than some of the other people here, so um but I never felt like we've ever been worried about being with this group or keeping up with the Jones' or anything like that. I guess the biggest pressure is like I said, significant people in my family to me, have been pretty successful in what they've done and I guess I feel pressure to try to match up with that. There was never any pressure that you have to do martial arts or do this or that.

My grandfather actually owns a steel fabrication business that he's been pretty successful and there is never really any pressure to join that. I've worked there several summers when I was home from school but I felt they were pretty open. I say that I kind of gravitated to physical athletic things my whole life. That's kind of where my interest was, I think probably because the rest of my family is competitive but I never felt like I had any pressure to have to do. It's just something that I wanted to do.

Anything I chose to do they would have been supportive of me and help me out with it. I would say hands on. My mother was a…she was much more hands on than my dad ever has been. She was very involved; not that my dad was hands off, but pushy is not the word, but some people could have accused her of being a helicopter parent. Definitely hands on.

PIVOTAL AND TURNING POINT EXPERIENCES IN CAREER

The biggest one that jumps to mind is when I was 17, my mom passed away. So when you have a family member die that's a big thing, so you know, that is probably the biggest one. I didn't finish college because I started bartending and making money, so I stopped going to class. Got real burnt out (working at the bar, grandfather's shop, and going to school) on that and came back. Then I wished I would have gotten my degree. And I was going for a degree in sports management, which is what I would have ended up doing here, basically. But I think that…I don't know how it would have been coming back here anyway but I don't know how it would have affected me if I would have gotten my degree. It's still a goal to go back and get it but I don't know when it's going to happen.

MAKING MEANING OF CAREER EXPERIENCES

I started teaching here and I've been teaching here for about six years. Guess I could be more powerful. I don't know how to rate it on a scale to 1 to 10 for you but I think there are times where I could be more assertive. And sometimes I don't, maybe take as much of a risk as I could just with different opportunities, but for the most part I think I'm, you know, doing what I want to do.

My very first job, other than just working around the house and working for my grandparents, I think it was 16, I had to have been 16 cause I was driving. I started life guarding one summer and then once summer got over, I got a job at an Italian food restaurant as a waiter and then the next summer I worked at the Italian food restaurant a little bit and wound up starting as a life guard and starting working for my grandfather. I worked in the shop there for the next three summers while I was at school. I worked for one year at a call center, we got like a center where you call and work for donations and that was probably my least favorite job ever. And then I started working at the bar. I worked at the bar for three years. Before I started working at the bar I came home for a year and took a year off school and taught classes here at night and worked at my grandfather's shop in the mornings and went back to school and started working, working at the bar. Got real burnt out on that and came back and started teaching here and I've been teaching here for about 6 years. Yes, since I was 13 and somewhere in there I was teaching in high school, my last year in high school.

CONTINUANCE OF THE LEGACY

Yeah, I don't think were done growing yet, I think there is still room to grow. I guess I'm training people who are going to want to stick around and become instructors or be successful in martial arts. And hopefully there are some kids that even if they don't stay with martial arts, they get some lessons about how to work hard and how to be focused and stay committed to something. Hopefully just what we're teaching them here it sticks with them and they have a positive influence on people.

The Blend of Families into the Legacy

THELMA'S STORY

Thelma Callagari said "My world was we were blending families, I was quitting a job that I was successful at to work with him and that was a huge step for me". Thelma, Clinton's wife, was energetic for a person who had her leg in a cast. She spoke of her disappointment with her current condition because the leg was preventing her from completing another black belt test; and this was important because her kids were passing her up due to her injury. From speaking with her, I could tell she is the heart of the business. She seemed at home with speaking with parents and kids coming into the school and with interacting with her son, Omar, who was just feet away. During the interview he sneezed and from behind her desk, she leans forward and yells "Bless you!" and waits for him to respond with "thank you" before she continues. I could see her happiness and her content with having her family nearby. Though Thelma was busy with the operations of the school, she took time out to sit with me and share her career story.

FAMILY BEGINNINGS
I pretty much raised myself. My grandmother, she passed away when I was 12 and then...I think my most admiration was my grandmother. She'd always pushed me to be whatever I wanted to be. During my time of growing up, it was a lot of controversy over women in the working environment but I was always told that whatever I wanted to do, to go for it and do it. I lived with my grandparents until I was 12 and then I lived with my mom.

EXISTENCE OF CAREER INFLUENCES AND ROLE MODELS
"Probably junior high, I wanted to be a school teacher". Thelma indicated that her family offered no career advice, guidance, or support. She mentioned Clinton was most influential in the development of her career identity.

My current husband, he pushed me to do what I loved the most. I lived with my grandparents until I was 12 and then I lived with my mom and she just, she had a good job because she worked from the bottom up. She didn't like what she did but she made good money. She worked for a dental office and it wasn't until she was much, much older that she got her real estate license and does very well and enjoys doing that. But watching her work really hard to provide for her family, is actually what I did. I started at companies from the bottom and worked my way to the top. So I guess she did inspire me in that way to if you have to start from the bottom and do everything, you can get to the top.

FAMILY VALUES
I mean it was not ever told I had to specifically do a certain career nor led to any certain career but told to choose whatever I wanted to do and be the best at it. To forgive and forget, to love one another; to work hard and be the best you can be.

These were the dominant values taught to her by her grandmother, whom she admired the most. She mentioned the only thing offered to her by her family was the expectation to graduate high school. Ironically, it was a high school teacher who provided consistent encouragement for her to become a teacher. Overall, Thelma's family values and support were intertwined to guide her into her career experiences.

PIVOTAL AND TURNING POINT EXPERIENCES IN CAREER
Well my grandmother died when I was 12 and that was a huge turning point for me. I wanted to be a school teacher but when I graduated from high school, college wasn't an opportunity. I really enjoyed martial arts and there was a time in my life where I couldn't afford it anymore... divorce. Three kids and a single mom it just wasn't happening. Then financial needs set in and I got a job at the mortgage company and worked my way to the top. When I met Clinton and I found out he was a martial arts school owner, I was so excited (laughs) yeah, that was a bonus. Then after we were married, I quit working and started with him. I was quitting a job that I was successful at to work with him and that was a huge step for me.

MAKING MEANING OF CAREER EXPERIENCES

I started at companies from the bottom and worked my way to the top. She'd [my grandmother] always pushed me to be whatever I wanted to be. I wanted to be a school teacher but when I graduated from high school, college wasn't an opportunity I had and so I thought that one day I'd get to college and I would do that. But the funny thing is that volunteering at the schools with my kids, I realized I could never be a school teacher because I would probably kill them all. (laughs) But in a martial arts environment, if you think about talking back to me I could say "give me 20 pushups" and that's acceptable. So in my heart I realized I wanted to be a teacher but I didn't realize of what. I assumed school but I very much enjoyed teaching martial arts, so it's a passion that diverted me a little bit but I got on the right path eventually. I just loved working with kids, still till this day I love working with kids.

When I was already doing martial arts where we met, my world was we were blending families. I was quitting a job that I was successful at to work with him and that was a huge step for me. (laughs) I really enjoyed martial arts. So I started training with him and he pushed me to do what I loved the most and we didn't have a Krav Maga course for women when we first opened the school together and that class teaches women how to protect themselves and that was my passion. So I've had extensive training and we've trained all of our staff to teach the Krav Maga extensively, to teach it to men and women. I go to schools and teach to junior high kids and I have Girl Scouts and Boy Scouts and they come here and learn from me and it's what I very much love to do and he pushed me to do what I love.

It was a better choice for my family because we were going from me working a lot outside of the home and spending little time with them to me being with them soon as they got out of school till they went to bed at night. Being able to take them to school and go to school plays and be more of a mom. But this environment we were running solely on us but they were involved in it. We grew this school from, it had 89 students when I started, 250 when we moved into this building. It was a good choice, I mean we work really good together and we involve our kids in everything we do and they work really good together. I'm in the right career choice. The older I got, it was important to me, to choose a career that I was happy doing and it makes me happy that my family is here.

I think success has to do with doing something you're happy with doing and doing something that's your gift that God gave you. I believe that if you're doing a gift that God gave you, it's something you were meant to be and it's something that makes your heart happy and it's something you enjoy doing. And that to me is being successful.

Helping kids and not just learning to protect themselves but to build their confidence and know they can be the best of themselves. This isn't a sport where you rely on the whole team to make it to the top but you just rely on yourself. So if you want to make it to the top, you can make it to the top and we encourage the kids to do that.

CONTINUANCE OF THE LEGACY

We encourage all of our students here, and so what I want... sorry it's gonna make me cry. (tears up) I want each of these (she reaches for tissue) 500 students or whatever that are here to leave a legacy. And I want to be a part of giving them the opportunity to (voice starts to change as she begins to cry) leave a legacy.

Thelma's compassion for her students, passion for teaching, and martial arts, and joy of working with her family spills over into her desire to incorporate her children in the legacy she is helping to build with her husband Clinton. After our interview, I then prepared to interview her son Omar.

OMAR'S STORY

One memorable statement that stood out to me from Omar was "I'm not a very goal-setting person, I don't have a lot. It's just kind of like...I go where the wind blows me and wherever I land, I land."

Omar is a tall, spirited 20 year old with his own style. The day I interviewed him, it was a hot summer day, in the 90's and he was there with a winter hat with flaps on the side that came down his head and he wore a t-shirt and shorts. I was not originally scheduled to interview him, but Clinton suggested I do so as Tobias was late arriving to the school and I had finished interviewing him and his wife already. Omar was eager to do the interview and Thelma swiftly told him to come into her office and she would go to the reception area to fill in for him until the interview was over. However, Thelma joined us for the interview, cleaning her desk, filing, and engaging in other work related tasks while I conducted the majority of the interview. Omar came around and sat behind the desk and our interview began.

FAMILY BEGINNINGS

My earliest career ambition… I want to say it's something to do with dogs. I think it might have been something with dogs, animals, uh, I don't know rescue, I just like dogs, I like training dogs. My dog is one of the most well trained dogs you'll ever meet. She knows all the tricks, every trick in the book. I was always pushed to try different things.

Family is weird. Both sides of my family are opposite and I do come from a split family. We had fake family history that my great grandma had lied about. We thought we were however much Native American and ended up we weren't.

EXISTENCE OF CAREER INFLUENCES AND ROLE MODELS

My grandpa…and it wasn't until I actual grew up that I realized how much of an important role he played in my life. He's one of the most kind, hardworking, smartest, most honorable men you'll ever meet.

[Regarding career identity], I would probably say Clinton, my stepdad, Master Callagari. He owns the business and he worked for a family business as well and he branched out and created his own business and is very successful. He's working on other stuff now and it's all entrepreneurial things he decided he wanted to do, so he did it and that's kind of what I want to do. My youth pastor, he led me to be a youth pastor through him and overtime he left and overtime it started going more to the little kids rather than the high school.

FAMILY VALUES

Just to keep good. Love the ones you hold dear, you know and try to keep as many good relationships and do your best to be honest and to love and be good to family members, you know. Intelligence but laziness and strength and good family values. On my mom's side, it's more so generosity, honesty, and love.

PRESSURE & SUPPORT

I don't like to let other people live my life for me. I don't live by traditions, if someone in my family has a bad relationship with someone else in the family, that doesn't transpire to me, even if it's my mom or my dad. My relationship with that person is completely separate and I'm going to try to keep it good as much as I can. So uh I wouldn't say there's necessarily an impact from someone else. So uh and

Pursuing Legacy

really just not much no real pressure. I'm very well supported. I try to keep good people in my life so that I don't get discouraged from things.

However, he offered a contradictory statement in regard to a career he had in professional gaming.

I pursued a career in gaming, which was looking promising but I didn't have support (laughs) so it kind of died off. Mom doesn't see a future with gaming, so mom doesn't support gaming. (laughs)

PIVOTAL AND TURNING POINT EXPERIENCES IN CAREER

Being kicked out of the house twice (looks at mom) (laughs) uh, leaving another house by choice. I think part of it is just growing up. I can recall and I talk about this all the time to people who talk to me about it. Um one time I was just driving in my truck, I was 18 years old, I'm 20, I turn 21 at the end of this month. I was just driving and I was thinking, I like to think a lot and I kind of hit this point where I was like, "hmmm." I started thinking about a lot of things, how what I did was not necessarily childish but as an 18 year old adult, things I shouldn't really, well I haven't gotten into any trouble. The last time I got into trouble was in 4th grade. Maybe 5th grade, I don't know I'm a kind of straight and narrow kind of person. But uh just childish things, like girls for example. Every guy is like "oh girls, whoo" but that time in my car when I was driving I thought "why was I wasting time?, you know". The time will come when I meet said girl and if something happens it happens, stop chasing them but it just happened but that is just one example. I mean, you, um, being more grown up about my relationships, I talked to people about how much they meant to me and just uh that was a big one for me. It was a thought that just happened to me.

I had a job and it was good and then I got kicked out. I'm putting in time to get the job that I want, so I went to do that. So when I did that, someone who was working here decided he was going to go back to his old job, so he put in his notice and my mom, and I'm living with them now, again, and I was living with her at the time and she was like "why don't you work for Full Force?"

MAKING MEANING OF CAREER EXPERIENCES

My very first job was actually here, um but it was janitorial work, I was cleaning windows, vacuuming floors. I think, so that was the first thing I did. Then I did, uh, I was working for a company making cellphone tutorials, using Java and Photoshop. Really at that time is what I really wanted to do, so for me to fall into that was huge and I was super grateful for that and not only did I have a job but I had a career at only 17 years old. I graduated high school early, I was out of school, I had job and it was good and then I got kicked out.

But so, I went from there to, I didn't have a job after a year after that, then I came back home. I was in Georgia for that. I came back and I worked at a movie theater, I worked at a summer camp, I worked at an afterschool care daycare. I was averaging about 100 hours a week, it was really draining on me. But then the job as the camp counselor, the daycare ended and I was just working at the movie theater. Um and got a job at an after school daycare and for me that was so much better than the movie theater. The movie theater was the worst job that I ever had and I can't imagine anything worse, it was honestly terrible.

And then I worked here and this is where I'm at now. And whatever, oh I did the gaming. I pursued a career in gaming, which was looking promising but I didn't have support (laughs) so it kind of died off. I was a professional gamer for a year and a half and obviously that's not something that your parents are usually supportive of, so..and I didn't make super great money off of that but I did make money. Um so I mean there's certain things they show support and certain things they don't. So it's just kind of where they see, you know…they don't see success in video games.

They see success in the family business for example. "Don't play video games, work for the family business!" (laughs and looks at mom) Parents want their kids to be successful and I guess pulling me in here, working closer to home, working for the family business, it's… I mean it's not only good for the business, I mean its family business, right? It's also, it's more ah comforting to my family because they know I am working, it's a steady job, I'm not going to get fired unless I do something drastic, right? (looks at mom) (laughs)

I'm not a very goal-setting person, I don't have a lot. It's just kind of like…I go where the wind blows me and wherever I land, I land. I cannot decide on anything. I'm very indecisive; I'm more of like a go with the flow kind of person. I'm very social, so any time I get to spend with people, spending time with people is a hobby for me. Um talking, I love talking. Most people when you think of hobby, talking doesn't come to mind but I love talking, I love entertaining, I love making people laugh. Um I love video games, it's something that I've always been good at, I enjoy doing and it's also another social aspect for me cause I play games with my friends and stuff.

Here he states love a lot but after he talks about other things, he says he likes them instead of love.

As far as economics, and getting into job security, like I said we don't have to worry about job security, it's a family business and if I mess up then I get to keep my job. (laughs) I like first off that it's a family business, it makes the atmosphere more comfortable. We own it and we do everything. For example, if I mess up at another job, the boss is like hammering you down. If I mess up here, my mom is not going to hammer me down, it's like 'you messed up, can you not mess up again?' and that hasn't come yet, luckily though, uh just if it does, I'm not going to get, and if it does, I have less of a risk being fired, more job security, which is nice. And then my job is very social, like I said, and I'm a social person.

I tried a lot of different things. I did volunteer work for my church, I played sports, I worked for the family business, and I've done a whole other things. I kind of was in a transfer period and that afterschool care and that summer job I had worked with the church camp, um they kind of were offering me something more. I wanted to put time into that and it was going to be volunteer work at first and be more permanent and the job would have branched off from that, but the way I looked at it you go to school to get a job, right? Well instead of going to school I was going to put in volunteer hours. First of all, I don't have to pay for it and second of all I'm putting in time to get the job that I want, so I went to do that.

So when I did that, someone who was working here decided he was going to go back to his old job, so he put in his notice and my mom, and I'm living with them now, again and I was living with her at the time and she was like "why don't you work for Full Force?" and I was like (sighs) like I cause, I kind of wanted to still put in the volunteer time and see what I could do with that but it wouldn't have worked with my schedule and at the same time, I do enjoy it here, you know, my job is very social cause I do all the signing up. So um it just kind of was an invitation that was fared out to me cause I was kind of in a transfer period and I took it and I enjoyed it.

I, myself have more of an entrepreneurial mind rather than, I don't want to say work a usual desk job. I do enjoy it here. I want to be making money um cause I want to move out, I want to be independent, and at the same time it was an opportunity to be a part of the family business, which I liked. Uh, but it was easy for me so there wasn't much going on in my life, there wasn't anything too difficult that would lead me from not taking it so it was kind of like an easy thing to do. And it made sense.

CONTINUANCE OF THE LEGACY

I'm a strong Christian believer, so I want to transfer my Christian values that shine through me into kids; show them how it's changed me and how it's led my life to be good. It's done something. Success to me is not just being alive but living. Being happy, having people around me, not necessarily being able to buy whatever I want or have as much money as I want, but to have strong relationships and to be surrounded by good people. I don't know necessarily what I want to leave for the next generation but I know I want to leave something whether it be just my knowledge or an ideal that I could set in the minds of them.

Chapter Summary

The Callagari family career legacy is one built on entrepreneurship and a hobby of this blended family. Clinton, a second generation steel fabrication businessman, has followed in the entrepreneurial footsteps of his father when he combined a childhood hobby and a family pastime into a family martial arts business. Now he is incorporating the ideals and business acumen of his father as he involves his children, his wife, and her children in the family business. Though there seemed to be a difference of opinions and perspectives, this family agreed on leaving a legacy not only for the next generation in their family but imparting their values, morality, and confidence in their students to guide their paths and help them to become productive members in society.

The Callagari family teaches us the following about developing a family career legacy:

1. Exemplify and promote the value of hard work.
   a. Tell and show family members and children the importance of hard work and tenacity.
2. Get children involved with the family business at an early age.
   a. Provide them with ownership opportunities and duties. Explain the importance of their responsibility and their level of

ownership and how it fits into the overall operation of the business.

b. Involve them in the various processes of the business, including the vision.

3. Communicate your expectations and plans for them to become heirs in the business.

4. Communicate and ensure the transfer of family values, business ethics, and business knowledge.

5. Support the career aspirations of children and family members, regardless of career decision.

a. Provide verbal and physical encouragement.

b. Provide financial and supportive resources (e.g. business networks, connections, mentorship, time, etc.)

c. Enroll them in programs that will help them to hone necessary skills for success in proposed career decisions.

d. Encourage them to pursue their passions and you seek to pursue yours.

6. Think generative in the provision for family living and in helping others in the community and abroad.

a. Select a career or business with a mission that expresses what you enjoy doing and believe in.

b. Select a career or business which will allow you to provide a living for your family.

c. Select a cause you are passionate about and that fits with your personal mission and career which will help improve the lives of others beyond your family. In doing so, involve your family in the process and activities of these community-focused efforts.

CHAPTER 7
THE ESSENCE OF LEGACY

As we saw from the examples in the previous chapters of this book, legacy is a multifaceted phenomenon comprised of traditions, values, experiences, and accomplishments woven into a reputation. This reputation is manifested into an identity where others connect their own aspirations, motivations, skillsets, and abilities to acceptable career roles, a term known as career identity. The career identity then becomes the foundation for the continuance of the family career legacy. That was a lot to process but it is important to know the terms to put the understanding of the family career legacy in perspective, so that you can begin to position your legacy for success. In fact, this chapter will help you to understand the essence of the family career legacy better by breaking it down based off the information shared by the family stories in the previous chapters. Then Chapter 8 will discuss how you can impose the tips given by these families to create and maintain your own family legacy.

In the introduction of this book, legacy was explained as a result of the McAdams generative state where an individual approaches middle-age and seeks to nurture and provide for future generations. What we learned from the commonalities in the career stories of the family members in the chapters, was generative thinking caused the formation of the legacy but there was other significance to the perpetuation of the legacy by family members before they reached middle-age. Mainly, it was career identity that served as a prominent factor in the desire to be associated and a contributor to the family career legacy.

Career Identity

Let's remember when speaking of family career legacies, family businesses and intergenerational careers are the direct result of these legacies. In this book's introduction, we learned that statistically, family business is the cornerstone of entrepreneurship and a major employer to the United States' workforce and contributor to the country's GDP. It is also responsible for a third of Fortune 500 companies and for producing political and social dynasties, such as the Kennedy, Bush, Jackson, Barrymore, and Hilton families, to name a few. From these internationally known legacies to the untold legacies in our local communities, the common denominator in the perpetuation of the family career legacy is career identity. It is the result of the influence the family has on career decisions which presents a deeper connection to generativity beyond McAdams' life stage. We learn familial influence provides a reasoning for following in the footsteps of family members because of a personal attraction to financial and psychological dependency. The continuation of a family business/intergenerational career in the third and fourth generations is often based on a desire to belong, the influence of the family, and their social identity, which is linked to their family and the prestige associated with the family name, business, and/or career, ergo career identity.

So let us explore career identity further using some of the examples given from the families in this book. From the stories, there was a strong association with social identity when dealing with families, as it is through the family structure and interaction patterns an individual began to create their career identity and understand their career decisions. This was prevalent in the statements about the family values. Rick Hankerton told a story of his grandfather teaching values to his father. Thus, his father told him the story to teach him values. This showed a pattern of family values in a story of business and career.

This was significant in building family values which included the element of business and how to treat employees, which is another pattern of career experiences. This was generative thinking for career, entrepreneurship, business leadership, and community involvement. Another way to look at it, is from the family values passed onto the participants by their parents or respective family members that were not only told to them but demonstrated through their parents' business interactions. Therefore, through the interactions with people, business successes and transactions, and sacrifices the participants witnessed from their role models were processed as a value system which they emulated and utilized as a benchmark in their careers. In other words, participants associated family values as business values, which led to their career identity in determining what it means to have a certain career.

For example, Patty Herrera spoke of her parents telling her to "do the right thing" as a child and she saw them following this manta in their business dealings. So in her banking career, part of her assessment of success as bank president and now chairman, was her reflecting on whether or not she made the right decision for the bank and for the people the bank serves. Even her initial career decision to return to the bank on a full-time basis after graduating from college, was based on her assessment of her skills and the position of where she could make the most impact in doing what she felt was right. Ultimately, she decided to return home to serve her community, which she felt was the right thing. This indicates the major influences on her career decisions and the development of her career identity.

Additionally, family interactions in career identity were also the explanation for the sense of community that was common in family career legacies. The fourth generation Hankertons mentioned their feelings on community being more effective in Pleasantville because of the established reputation of the family name and social identity in the town. Remember Kevin stated "I wanna be known as someone who gave back to the community he was born in". This was how Rick identified his career and legacy of community involvement. Kevin's father, Sam, made the connection for his career identity to be fully exercised and for him to meet the family benchmark of being recognized for community involvement in an atmosphere appreciative of his skills, interests, and motivations.

Additionally, Tobias Callagari admired his father and grandfather for their entrepreneurial successes; however, he seemed apprehensive to make solid career decisions and in the opinion of his father Clinton, he was not taking enough ownership in the business. The diagnostic was that Tobias was comparing his success to his father's and grandfather's successes; thus, from his perspective he had not measured up to what it meant to be an entrepreneur, according to how he viewed his role models (his father and grandfather). Therefore, it was not a question of whether he wanted to take ownership in the business but for Tobias, his career decisions had not matched his career identity. He was looking for a way to take ownership of the business but with his own impression. His gravitation to martial arts because of his interest in athletics and competitive sports, was his way of measuring himself to his family and that was why he felt withdrawn to the point he noticed differences between himself and certain family members. He was not exactly sure how he could make his own impact and thus had no career identity of his own, from his perspective.

These examples show us the importance of family values in career identity and how individuals view their parents as role models providing insight on how they have constructed their career identity and how the family's value system is used in making career decisions. This indicates their aspirations and whether or not they were satisfied with said decisions. We will discuss role models more in Chapter 8, but it is significant to see how family values are perpetuated to influence career decisions through associated identity. Career identity is how people see themselves in the future, in more of an aspiration of how they want to be identified. Therefore the career identity in legacies serves as an umbrella, whereas the family members share a career identity and seek to find their part in that identity by assessing their own identity to see if it fits within the perceived family career identity.

The familial influence on career identity is the last point I want to discuss on this topic before I introduce a model that shows you the dynamics of a family career legacy and how generative thinking fuels the legacy. Throughout this chapter and in previous chapters, the familial influence has been demonstrated and insinuated through the career stories and discussion of said stories, but I wanted to draw attention to this influence directly. The familial influence, meaning what parents and other family members who serve as role models for an individual, is a strong force in career decision making for various reasons. For example, Clinton Callagari referred to his father as "undisputedly the best in the business in the world" as one of the reasons he started his own business and believed he was the only one out of his siblings who had the business sense to run his father's family business. Clinton proclaimed to have the same business acumen as his father, which was demonstrative of the influence his father had on his career identity and career choices.

Rick Hankerton recalled a remark a fellow board member made about how the Hankerton family tended to "reload", meaning they trained the next generation to participate in the same social activities and that next generation carried the ideals from the previous generation. Rick acknowledged several family patterns and spoke frequently about what his father did and how he followed in the same path. Though he stated he was the main influence on his own career identity, it was clear his father was a major influence because he modeled his career path and community involvement. This was evident in the other generations of the Hankerton family as well, in essence their career identity provided guidance of how they were to perform socially.

In Richey Don's case, we see how the familial influence on career identity works in reverse. It is important to note Richey Don had many jobs which contributed to his career identity as a businessman. Richey's career story revealed his many occupations, which contributed and prepared him for entrepreneurship and a legendary career as a DJ. The various skills acquired through childhood and adulthood occupations formed his career identity. Richey frequently referred to himself as a businessman from the time he was younger, stating "I was a businessman from the get go". This was actually him processing his career identity. He made references to his ability to make money, which meant he measured success with the amount of money he made. This was key in his story where he made many comparisons between rich people and poor people. In fact, he compared his two sets of grandparents, his father's side as middle-class and his mother's side as poor. He then stated how he loved spending time with his paternal family because of their middle-class lifestyle. Also, the other people he admired, as a child, were financially sound and owned businesses in the town, which were representative of his aspirations and validation for success. Thus when he began to help his son's career by purchasing a funeral home, the familial influence on career identity worked in reverse.

The career stories of the family members provided insight on the importance of career identity to their legacies. Therefore understanding individual career identity provides insight into the career decision making process and the role the family plays in the decision to become involved with the legacy. This demonstrates how career identity is rooted in the family and careers are co-constructed by families. This is important for you to understand to begin to position yourself and family to create a legacy. Now we will build on the dynamic of career identity and see how legacies are created, experienced, and maintained through the explanation of the legacy model.

The Legacy Model

The legacy model (Figure 7) is a framework for how family career legacies are created, experienced, and maintained. I developed this model in 2013 as part of an original study and found it to be helpful as a competency model to better understand family career legacies. I have included examples from the stories shared in previous chapters to add further clarification for how the model works and the dynamic of family legacies. The model suggests the social cohesion between and within generations creates a constant exchange of support through stories and encouragement. Social cohesion was demonstrated in the stories shared by the families in this book relying on their family for career advice, support of career aspirations and decisions, and development of career identity through the family relationship and environment. The constant exchange of support between family members equates to the familial influence on career choices and decisions and through role modeling and the creation of a network. So let's look at this concept as defined in the third box from the top of the model in Figure 7.

The intergenerational solidarity and ambivalence theory grounds this social cohesion and sets patterns in this phase. For example, in the Hankerton family, Trey considered himself to be blessed because of the foundation his family had established. The stories told by his father Rick and other family members from other generations conveyed the journey in establishing this foundation, which exemplified this type of social exchange. In another example, as children, Melissa Ortiz and her cousins had to read the newspaper with their grandfather before they could play. As a group, he would quiz them on what they read and this embedded a habit of staying abreast of current events and increased family interaction with the discussion of said events.

The family's social cohesion then affects the family social capital or the creation of the social structure, which is defined in the fourth box

Figure 7: The Legacy Model

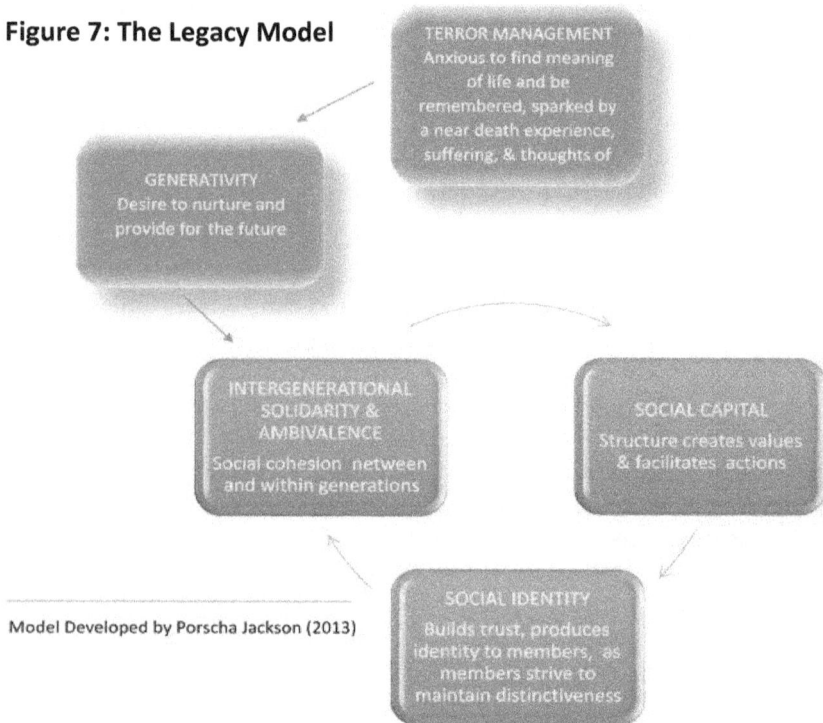

TERROR MANAGEMENT
Anxious to find meaning of life and be remembered, sparked by a near death experience, suffering, & thoughts of

GENERATIVITY
Desire to nurture and provide for the future

INTERGENERATIONAL SOLIDARITY & AMBIVALENCE
Social cohesion between and within generations

SOCIAL CAPITAL
Structure creates values & facilitates actions

SOCIAL IDENTITY
Builds trust, produces identity to members, as members strive to maintain distinctiveness

Model Developed by Porscha Jackson (2013)

138

to the right. Essentially, the family structure is the center of social capital. During this stage the family value system and beliefs are nurtured and imparted to generations. Because of the closeness of the family, families begin to co-construct the values, through trust and respect, necessary in their careers and the business. The construction of a value system was illustrated in the Hankerton family with how John told the story to Richard about how to treat employees during a layoff, which is ultimately the set of values the Hankerton family abides by today. The story told by John, was passed down through generations and provided a structure for how the family was to govern themselves. Rick documented this system in the books that he authored, intentionally to ensure his grandchildren and future generations understood the family value system. Rick's actions showed a pattern of family values and the story was told in the facet of business and career. This was significant in building family values that included the element of business and how to treat employees, which is another pattern of career experiences. These actions were demonstrative of generative thinking for career and entrepreneurship, business leadership, and community involvement.

The fifth component to the model is social identity theory, which is defined as the maintenance of a distinction by a particular group. This is where family members make meaning of their family career legacy experience and how they will contribute to it in an effort to perpetuate the legacy within their community and distinguish their value system and their family business from others. In the Whitney family, Ned demonstrated a uniqueness of his family through his prideful statements of his grandmother studying under pioneer Madame CJ Walker and being a successful female entrepreneur during an oppressive time period. He boasted his family's accomplishments were "astronomical" because of them being the first Black cosmetology school in the state and still a viable competitor, despite the influx of corporate-owned beauty schools. This was an example of social identity, by having the need to associate with family because of a distinguishing characteristic.

Let me explain this concept further. Remember in the Hankerton family, Kevin stated he wanted to move back to Pleasantville from the larger metropolitan city to make a greater community impact because of his family's reputation in the town? He proudly stated "Banking to my family is so much stronger than banking to probably 95% of families out there because of the legacy that is here 'cause of the family that is here." In the Jones family, Todd Jones differentiated his family's funeral home from others by dispelling the negative connotations that came with being involved in the funeral business. These examples follow the presented legacy model because it is the social identity created from the social capital. These two theories set the foundation of the family values and this is consistent with the Jones brothers' (Todd and Jordan) statement on continuing the legacy of their father's (Richey Don) career reputation. Therefore, the social identity goes into the intergenerational solidarity and exchange as a harbor for family interaction for future generations. This results in exactly what the Jones brothers hope for their children.

Furthermore, families determine how, through their individual career contributions, they will perpetuate the legacy for future generations; a maintenance leading back to the intergenerational social cohesion and support exchange. For the Hankerton family, Trey was groomed by his father to be Vision Bank's president. Throughout his career he worked with other organizations to gain the knowledge and experience to bring back to Vison Bank. Now as president, he and his father Rick are planning Trey's son's entry into the bank through the stories and experiences they are sharing with him as a child. For the Whitney's, Shirley expressed several times the pride she had, marrying into the third generation, with being associated with the accomplishments of the family business. This was representative of social identity and her goal to pass on the Whitney value system and encourage future generations to follow in her footsteps. This example of social identity feeding back into the legacy model with the intergenerational solidarity and ambivalence theory.

As you can begin to see more strategically how the family career legacies work through the model, I hope you are understanding the role stories play in furthering the legacy. Essentially, the stories we tell become the vehicle that transports the value systems and identity from one generation to the next. Contained in the stories are life-altering and social experiences told from the perspective of how we have made meaning of such experiences.

This now brings us to the first (terror management theory) and second (generativity) boxes in the legacy model, which ignite the creation of the family career legacy. It is at this moment the model begins as we see the importance of generative thinking and how it fuels the entire process because of its need to provide for future generations, be immortalized, make an impact in their communities through activities and compassion, and perpetuate a particular set of values. As demonstrated by the Herrera family, their legacy was created in response to a disruptive event experienced by Armando Herrera, who was not able to get a loan because of his ethnicity.

This could have been the case for some of the other first generation members of families in this study; however, most of them were deceased at the time of the research. I can imagine this was the case for the Whitney family as Madame Crawford was a Black woman in an era where women had limited job opportunities and Blacks had limited freedoms due to oppressive and discriminatory circumstances. In response of the disruptive events, like the passing of his wife and 9/11, in the Callagari family, Clinton Callagari started his martial arts business. Situations such as those experienced by Armando, Madame Crawford, and Clinton became the primary reason for making generative career decisions, which may be best explained through the terror management theory. This theory suggests a person's near death experience or exhaustion of challenging experiences drives them to create a better life for their loved ones. It is then from this life-altering experience, they realize the fragility of life and move toward creating a legacy that will outlive them through their impact, which is revered and carried on through their offspring. In essence, legacy is proof your life mattered.

Summary

This chapter shared with you the overall meaning of family career legacy, the basis of its origin, what it is in the perspective of the family career or business, how much it is tied to identity (specifically career identity), what factors are key to its maintenance, and how it operates. I hope the use of the specific examples from the families provided further clarification in your understanding of the essence of legacy. My goal was to get you to look a bit deeper into legacy and discover the various facets and how those facets come together to build and continue a legacy.

CHAPTER 8
BUILDING YOUR LEGACY

Throughout this book, I have strived to give you a better glimpse at legacy through the real-life stories of persons who have created, experienced, and maintained a successful legacy throughout multiple generations. I have coined the term family career legacy as a way to denote a specific legacy that is depicted in family businesses and intergenerational careers. From the examples given and discussed in Chapters 1-6, you can better understand the importance of stories and story-telling in this process. Furthermore, through the chapter summaries which highlight the key components to family career legacy and the explanation of how these legacies work through the legacy model, as described in chapter 7, you should have a greater understanding and appreciation for family career legacies. In this final chapter, I will discuss the major components, shared in this book, of a legacy in terms of helping you to begin to build your own, whether you seek to pursue a family career legacy or just your personal legacy.

Five Basic Principles of Legacy

Building a legacy, as demonstrated through the shared stories and the legacy model, is a process. Beyond the competency of how the family career legacy works, the key principles of legacy are a strong set of values, mentorship, community involvement, family comradery, and generativity. These five are the basics of what each family shared in their stories and what was summarized from each of the chapters. Once you begin to implement these five principles, many other characteristics will come into play and spawn from these foundations.

Secondly, please keep in mind your career. Your career should reflect your passions, abilities, and most importantly, your purpose. The various jobs you have had should be either a linear or conglomerate journey to a meaningful career. Now I know employment is sometimes out of our control, believe me I've been there, but the permanent jobs you have should each be chapters in your overall career story. So what I'm saying to you, that to be in pursuit of legacy, you first must be in a position or field that is meaningful to you. How you make your job meaningful, is your own business, but you should be making an impact wherever you are. If you are not, then I encourage you to see a career coach or read some literature to help you exercise your options and find ways to seek purposeful employment and/or meaningful tasks within your current position. Regardless your employment status, I believe these five principles can help you to begin to think generatively, which is a step in the direction of legacy. So let's get into it!

Identify and Uphold Family Values

Values are qualities, characteristics, and principles we use as moral, ethical, as performance guides and standards. They are driving forces that guide our behavior and interactions in life. They are what is important to us, what we cherish, what we believe, and what we look for in others with whom we seek to build relationships. Because values are what we hold dear, they essentially are the core of who we are as individuals. Similarly, family values are the cornerstone of who we become; they are the base which forms our identity. It is our values

144

that set the precedence of what we believe, how we behave and react, and what we perceive as important. Hard-working, dignity, compassionate, persistence, and honesty are just a few examples of the family values shared by the family members in this book.

I am sure you could begin to list your personal values and in doing so, trace their origins back to specific qualities, sayings, mantras, experiences, and actions exemplified by members of your family. In fact, this is what I would advise you to do; think about your early family interactions and make a list of those values which come to mind. Also, start a list of your personal values; recall your pivotal personal and professional experiences. Take it a step further, examine the most important relationships you have with people and pinpoint what you admire, appreciate, aspire, and overall what attracts you to them. In building friendships, we often look for those who have the same values as us and therefore, you can identify your values by identifying the values of those you love and are around the most. On the flip side, we sometimes seek relationships with those who have values we wished we had and disassociate ourselves from those who represent the opposite of what we value or who we desire to be.

These are all ways to jumpstart the reflection process, so you can begin to identify your personal and familial values. To help you, I have included a value worksheet (Appendix A) that I hope you will find useful in completing this task. Identifying these values is the first step in building a legacy. It also helps in maintaining a legacy because it brings the family on one accord and guides visions, missions, interactions, career choices, community involvement, and family business ethics and operations. Remember what you value becomes a tale of who you are and that will be evident in the legacy you leave. I encourage you to reflect and list your values as presented in the worksheet and begin to think generatively about what values you want to pass on to your children, the community and world, whom you will make an impact on. Think about it, what do you want people to say about you, when you are not around? I will tell you, they will talk about what you valued because that will be what drives your relationships, accomplishments, successes, failures, experiences, and how others have experienced you.

Identify Role Models and Become a Role Model

Values cannot exist by themselves but must be demonstrated and upheld by someone. Often, the values we seem to cherish are those displayed by the people we admire and love, we call them role models. Role models were present in all of the career stories shared in this book. The majority of the family members claimed their parents as their primary role models, which is to be expected in a book about family career legacies. Through generativity, the significance role models have on the experience and maintenance of family career legacies is understood. What we learned is family, mainly parents and secondly those members who were in close contact with participants, served as career informants, motivators, and supporters who were instrumental in the formation of self-concept and the development of an interdependent environment which guided career decisions and academic pursuits. Parents' generative thinking resulted in preparation for the future through grooming efforts for successful careers in the family business. Parents used their position as role models to communicate acceptable and unacceptable careers and to promote career and academic expectations suitable to the family career legacy.

Families were supportive of any career decision with reason but those interested from a young age began the grooming process to continue the legacy as the previous generations set the example and had the next generation to shadow them in the early years. During their careers, they were building on previous generations to do better so the next generation would have a stable foundation set for success. This aided in the patterning of the upcoming generations.

Role models' actions outside of their careers served as illustrators of the acceptable behavior and character of a person with that career; thus, contributing to the development of career identity of participants. Therefore, role models began to construct the careers of the next generation by enforcing acceptable career and academic pursuits by example and by exposing them to the career at an early age, but not with significant pressure but as a possibility. Through this approach, role models were instilling values and interests that contributed to their career identity consisting of the family's social identity needed to sustain the family business. As such, through role models, the family career legacy was experienced and maintained through the patterning of the role model's career by the next generation.

So what this means is in building your legacy or contributing to your legacy, you, respectively, must decide to become a role model and identify someone who possesses the same values as you and/or has a career or legacy you aspire. Role modeling helps to create and perpetuate patterns for legacy; therefore, you must be cognizant of the behavior and actions you display. You must even be conscious of the activities you engage in and your association with people and organizations because they are all being watched and replicated. You see, role modeling becomes the basis for a lot of the legacy keys that were shared at the end of the previous chapters, such as: grooming others for the business; setting career expectations for children; involving family members in the business; and communicating and co-constructing family and business values and acceptable careers.

In preparing for the principle of role modeling, I have provided a worksheet example (Table 1) to help you chart possible role models. A clean version of the worksheet also exists in the appendix (Appendix B). Additionally, here are a few questions I hope you will find useful in acquiring a role model and preparing to be a role model.

- How would you define a role model?
- Who are your role models and why?
  - o List five characteristics that you admire about each of them.
  - o What are their accomplishments?
  - o Describe their reputation among others.
  - o What is their career? How are they involved in the community?
  - o Do they help others? How?
  - o What are your fondest memories of this person(s)?
- Who has impacted your life? How?
- What do you aspire to become?
- How do others view you? What's your reputation?
- What career do you want to have? Is there someone who has the same career you would like? Is there someone who has accomplished something you would like to accomplish?

- What aspects of your role models would you like to pattern yourself after?
- What's the most important quality a role model must have?
- How are you similar to your role model?
- What can you work on to become a role model for someone else?
- Who looks up to you? Who do you provide for or may have to provide for in the future?
- What impact do you hope to make on the community, nation, or world? Who has made this impact already?
- Whose career goals are most aligned to yours?
- Who has influenced your career decisions? How and why?

Table 1: Role Model Worksheet Example

About Me	Role Model 1 Name: Janay Roll	Role Model 2 Name: Ty James
My Anticipated Occupation: Teacher **My Anticipated Volunteer/Professional Position(s):** Teacher's Association, church children's program	**Occupation:** Real Estate Agent Community Involvement/Positions: Salvation Army Board, Church Usher	**Occupation:** Business Owner Community Involvement/Positions: Boy Scout troop leader, NBA All-star Weekend Volunteer Nat'l Association of Accountants
Characteristics/Qualities: Patient, hard-working, compassionate, energetic	**Characteristics/Qualities:** Hardworking, compassionate, efficient, driven, resourceful	**Characteristics/Qualities:** Organized, polite, respected, open-minded, problem-solver, always positive, encouraging
Values: Family, children, the future, honesty	**Values:** Family, community, public service, self	**Values:** Children, helping others, environment sustainability, education, hard-work
Aspired Accomplishments or Goals: Graduated college	**Aspired Accomplishments or Goals:** Started non-profit, received sales award from job, served 20years in military	**Aspired Accomplishments or Goals:** Volunteer of the year, father, honorary degree
Mantra: Work hard, play hard	**Mantra:** "If at first you don't succeed, try and try again"	**Mantra:** "Success is obtained when opportunity meets preparation"
Other:	**Other:**	**Other:**

Get Involved in the Community

Role models played a significant role in the career influences of the participants' career decision making and the construction of their careers. Through role modeling, many career patterns were formed and followed which resulted in the development of career identity. In the career stories of this book, a commonality of the participants' role models and for some, even the role model's role model, was their involvement in the community. This was an interesting factor because all of the families interviewed possessed a strong sense of community and belonging to something greater as part of who they are and as an element of their career. In essence, they selected careers which gave them a sense of belonging.

Getting involved in the community is a way to exercise who we are by doing the work for causes, issues, and people who truly speak to our heart, personal interests, and our very existence. Community involvement and service provides us with an intimate connection and a sense of belonging because our purpose in that moment is to serve others. It is in true servitude that we become selfless and exercise our own humanity by realizing all humans are interconnected and we must support each other, especially those less fortunate. Additionally, through our own service we can further humanity by bringing about change to our local communities and the world through our political and spiritual stances, economic and educational development and contributions, awareness, and time. I know it's a bit cliché to say "we are the world" but it is the truth. The essence of community service is realizing this concept that we (humans) are all in this world together and an issue that affects one of us, essentially affects us all. This is where we become connected to certain causes and gain our sense of belonging because we begin to empathize with others and want better for them.

In the stories, we witnessed community involvement from the simplicity of buying school supplies for community children to its pinnacle of fighting to bring racial and economic equality. What we learn is service to our community defines the essence of who we are and our careers and family businesses are the economic branches which fund our involvement and give us leverage for social and generational change, which perpetuates family career legacy. Therefore, as community involvement and service becomes a part of our daily existence, it becomes an engrained family value that links the family to the community.

The community service at times was more than just a commitment or part of the family value system, but it was also perceived as a career and as part of one's career identity. As such, when you are forming or maintaining your family career legacy, begin to think about how you can contribute and change your community for the better. You must realize that is business, it is the community who supports you and you must have a social responsibility to support them, it is reciprocity. Furthermore, community involvement strengthens your business and legacy by providing social networks and connections and enhancing your reputation. It solidifies your legacy in the community. Therefore, get your family involved in giving back, remember you have to set the example as a role model. If you are not a role model yet, this is another way for you to find an appropriate one by asking them about their community involvement.

Develop a Strong Family Relationship

This next principle piggy backs on the previous principle regarding serving the community. Developing a strong family relationship begins with passing on family values, but it also includes doing things together as a family as one of its key components; one way to do that is through community service. As an individual, there are a multitude of ways to give back: serving through volunteer organizations, contacting nonprofit organizations of interest and donating your time, serving on nonprofit and/or school boards, volunteering at your local schools, becoming a member of community service organizations, serving in ministry at your church, participating in holiday service events, and starting your own nonprofit organization and/or foundation, to name a few. There are many ways I have seen this done from a family standpoint. Here are a couple: feeding the hungry by adopting a family during the holidays, starting a family-run nonprofit organization/foundation, conducting drives (food, clothing, specific items for a certain group, etc.) for a certain cause, scheduling a day to serve the local community while on vacation, going on mission trips, and establishing scholarships. Really, what is done as a family can be done by an individual, but it has a greater impact as a group. Serving together helps to build the family's social identity (as discussed in the legacy model) because it reinforces the family values by creating an association with the family reputation and a social platform. Furthermore, it helps set expectations for future familial generations.

I know the next couple of sentences will sound repetitive, because it is, but I want you to understand it is an extremely crucial piece of information; so here goes. You must remember what you do in the community is a major part of your legacy, which exemplifies a deep sense of belonging. Getting involved in the community as a family helps to create a close family relationship and a greater impact, which is needed to have a successful family career legacy. It is the comfort in belonging to a tight-knit family, one where support, resources, and success are prevalent and members operate together as a unit. The participants shared there was no one individual's accomplishments but one person's accomplishment was an achievement for the family and there was an expectation for members to contribute to the family legacy and a desire among participants to make a worthy contribution to the legacy. The close relationship of the families and the values that were passed on also created an environment that promoted community. The accomplishments, procedures, and perspectives were represented holistically as a family and not individually.

The development of a tight-knit family means to create an environment of inclusion. Start to share your experiences with your children, introduce them to your hobbies, tell them childhood and family stories, visit family members, include them in your career, listen and discuss their aspirations, encourage them, and discover things together. Additionally, begin to do things as a family on a continuous basis, even when the kids are young, whether it's taking an annual family trip, having a monthly family date night, playing games together, participating in extracurricular activities (i.e. sporting teams, cooking classes, etc.) or whatever and wherever your imagination takes you. As you begin to do activities together, you will think of more things and find causes all of you are passionate about. Spending this time together creates a comradery that will bring you closer, perpetuate values, set expectations, start and continue traditions, build trust, and create learning experiences and long-lasting memories.

Think Generatively

Understanding the importance of having a tightly knit family brings us to generative thinking, the underlying principle for legacy. Remember, we discussed generative thinking in Chapter 8 as part of the Legacy Model. Generative thinking or generativity is where we not only think about how our actions, careers, associations, and decisions will affect future generations, but it is how we nurture and prepare these generations. The families in this book benefitted from the knowledge and resources of the previous generations and felt more powerful as individuals and more secure in their career because the legacy that had preceded them. (Appendix C has a family career tree to help you chart out your family's careers.) Additionally, the previous generations desired to provide a solid career foundation so future generations would not have to struggle and would have a career opportunity to fall back on. These actions were generative in thinking.

The earlier generations of these family career legacies approached their careers with the thought of being successful and leaving a good reputation for their children. This was evident with Richard Hankerton, who communicated to Rick in his final days that he had left him a good name and regardless of his career decision, he needed to maintain that good name for future generations. This was also demonstrated through Richey Donovan, who built a tremendous legacy in business and radio and had the desire to leave a business opportunity for his son and did so with the funeral home, though he originally wanted to leave Todd one of his existing businesses. Richard's and Richey's generative thinking was not only to provide for the next generation but to immortalize their career accomplishments through reputations and family value systems. This is indicative of how family career legacies are created.

The generativity of early generations create the basis for the legacy by providing the foundation of a value system, which builds character and guides behavior and career decisions. The ability of the legacy to hold a reputation and status in the community, further creates an environment of a proven career path that is nurtured and a supportive network of family where decisions are made together and success and failures are experienced together. Therefore, a person has the ability to make a greater impact in society through community involvement efforts as a group on the premise of proven accomplishments of family members. Essentially, one has the advantage because the path of involvement and participation has already been outlined and as generations emerge, the amount of career barriers decrease.

What this means for you is now is the time to activate your generative thinking. Whether you have children, a family or aspire to one day, you can begin to map out how you will make an impact in your community or world. This also is true for those of you who have no interest in having a family of your own but are interested in learning more about legacy. The only difference is in creating a family career legacy, you are including family in your plans and relying on the link from past to present.

If you are heeding to the other four basic principles, you will have already started the process of generative thinking. Whether it is a life-altering experience, as explained in the Legacy Model that propelled you to this point, or you just reached a pivotal time where you want to make impactful strides in your life, you can embrace the concept of thinking generatively. We are at a day and time where people are seeking meaningful lives and purposeful careers. Many scholars have attributed this to the changes in our economy over the past three decades. Richard Feller and Judy Whichard stated economic and job instability, technological advances, outsourcing, and a move toward a global economy has led to a change in how business is done and how people are approaching their careers and family. Also, I would have to add the recent social injustices our nation and world is facing, is another motivator for purposeful careers.

With this being said, thinking generatively has become a 21st century jewel in helping people to not only seek meaning and purpose in what they do but also how they will leave a legacy. Start your generative thinking by asking yourself and answering the following: What impact do I want to make in this world?; What do I want to be known for?; What do I want others to remember or say about me?; What is my purpose?; What do I hope to accomplish on my job and/or in my career?; How do others perceive me?; What does my talent or gift offer to the world?; How will my community be better off because of my work?; How can I help others?; What will I leave to others who will come behind me?; The world/my community/my job/my family is better off because I did ____; I have helped ____ because I have ____; What will my legacy be?; What aspects of my job are fulfilling?; How can I get more fulfillment in life by offering my talents, gifts, and knowledge?; How is what I do professionally and personally meaningful to me and to the community?; How am I providing for future generations?; and What can I do to provide, help, and change things for future generations?

Yes, thinking generatively begins with asking yourself a multitude of questions to get the process started. Your answers to those questions should be a gauge of your level of fulfillment and purpose. Remember, Todd and Jordan Jones spoke about their careers as being spiritual callings. This is achieved when you can identify and pursue your purpose. The spirituality part is realizing we as humans are all interconnected and everyone has a unique purpose and if we all operate within that purpose, which encompasses our natural talents and passion, then we achieve fulfillment. Not only do we feel what we are doing is meaningful to us, but it essentially becomes a blessing to others. Understanding this concept, leads us to be generative in what we are doing because we not only seek to make our surroundings better but through our actions effect change and make an impact. In doing this, and following the other four principles, we create our legacy. In essence, generative thinking occurs on many levels, in our personal, professional, familial, and communal lives. The beauty of it all is that these four facets are intertwined and work together through our persistence to achieve legacy.

Conclusion

This book scratches the surface to legacy and I hope intrigued your interest in this phenomenon. I also hope you have begun to think of legacy differently and it will propel you to approach your career with the intent of building and/or contributing to a legacy for yourself and/or your family. Additionally, I hope you understand the importance of the stories you tell. Stories are the vehicle in which our legacy travels; therefore, I hope you received an appreciation for stories and how you make meaning of your experiences to then communicate them to influence future generations. Furthermore, with reading the career stories of the families and then understanding the process of a legacy through the Legacy Model and the five principles of legacy, I hope you are inspired and realize the importance of creating a positive family environment, one that is rich in communication, support, love, compassion, and regular internal and external interaction.

In closing, your pursuit to legacy begins with your story. You must keep in mind that while you are living, you have the opportunity to continuously write, tell, and defend your story…your legacy. However, when you are gone, what you have done and achieved speaks for itself and through the experiences and words of others. What will they say about you when you are gone? Be blessed and pursue your legacy!

APPDENDIX

Appendix A

VALUES IDENTITY CHART

Values are the deep desires for how we interact and relate to ourselves and others in every situation we encounter in our personal, professional, and social lives. Deeply rooted in our foundational upbringings of parents, family, school, church, friends, etc., values consist of every experience and happening that has occurred in our lives. Our values are demonstrated in our everyday and work behaviors, decision making, and associations.

Values are the key to building and maintaining a legacy. This grid will help you to begin to identify your values, which will assist you in creating a solid foundation for your legacy. Use the following questions to help you start the process of identifying your values. Feel free to jot your answers down or just meditate on your responses to the questions. Who has inspired you and what qualities do they possess? What traits do you admire in others? To understand you, what do others need to know? What do you NOT tolerate in the actions and dealings with others? What is your passion(s)? What infuriates you? What were you told over and over again while growing up? What do you plan to pass on to the next generation?

The list of words below is available to help you with the following chart. Select the ones that are most important to you or add your own values, if not listed.

Altruism	Forgiving	Open-minded
Beauty	Freedom	Order
Business	Friendship	Organized
Career	Fun	Patient
Charity	Happiness	Peaceful
Community	Hard-working	Politics
Compassion	Harmony	Religious
Consistency	Home	Respect
Cooperative	Honest	Responsible
Courageous	Hopeful	Risk-taking
Creativity	Independent	Self-aware
Dependability	Intelligence	Self-Loving
Education	Logical	Service
Effective	Loving	Spiritual
Efficient	Loyal	Stable
Empathy	Materials	Strength
Ethical	Modesty	Structure
Family	Morals	Success
Fellowship	Nature	Superiority
Financial Security	Nutrition	Sympathy
Food	Obedience	Teamwork
Trustworthy	Victorious	
Understanding	Wealth	

	CAREER	COMMUNITY	EDUCATION	FAMILY	RELATIONAL	SOCIAL	SPIRITUAL
Pick two words to describe your performance or quality characteristics in each category							
Pick two words to describe your communication style with people in each category							
Choose one word to describe your decision-making style in each category							
Write the mantra/saying that comes to mind for each category							
List the values needed to maintain the above mantra							
Group similar values listed under each category and select the word that best captures what you value							
Rank each category in order of importance to you, with "1" being the most important to you							

Appendix B

ROLE MODEL WORKSHEET

About Me	Role Model 1 Name:	Role Model 2 Name:	Role Model 3 Name:	Role Model 4 Name:
My Anticipated Occupation: My Anticipated Volunteer/Professional Position(s):	Occupation: Community Involvement/Positions:	Occupation: Community Involvement/Positions:	Occupation: Community Involvement/Positions:	Occupation: Community Involvement/Positions:
Characteristics/Qualities:	Characteristics/Qualities:	Characteristics/Qualities:	Characteristics/Qualities:	Characteristics/Qualities:
Values:	Values:	Values:	Values:	Values:
Aspired Accomplishments or Goals:	Accomplishments:	Accomplishments:	Accomplishments:	Accomplishments:
Mantra:	Mantra:	Mantra:	Mantra:	Mantra:
Other:	Other:	Other:	Other:	Other:

Appendix C

FAMILY CAREER TREE

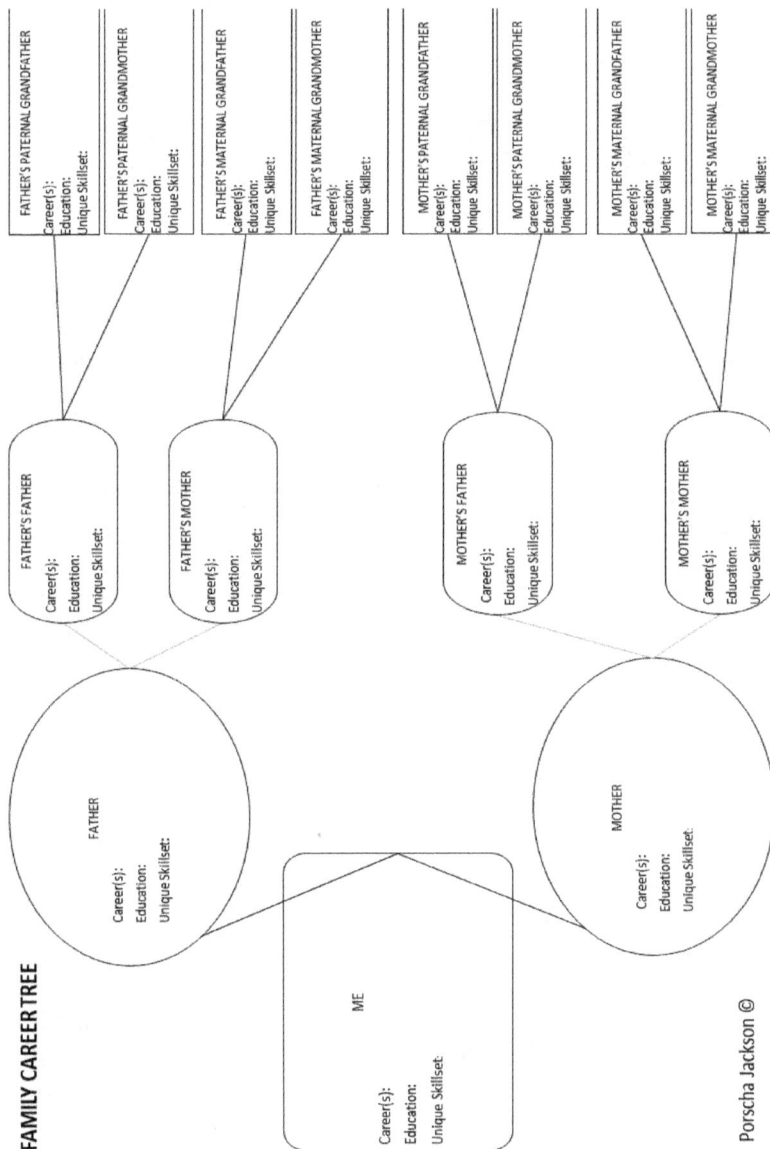

FAMILY CAREER TREE

FATHER'S PATERNAL GRANDFATHER
Career(s):
Education:
Unique Skillset:

FATHER'S PATERNAL GRANDMOTHER
Career(s):
Education:
Unique Skillset:

FATHER'S MATERNAL GRANDFATHER
Career(s):
Education:
Unique Skillset:

FATHER'S MATERNAL GRANDMOTHER
Career(s):
Education:
Unique Skillset:

MOTHER'S PATERNAL GRANDFATHER
Career(s):
Education:
Unique Skillset:

MOTHER'S PATERNAL GRANDMOTHER
Career(s):
Education:
Unique Skillset:

MOTHER'S MATERNAL GRANDFATHER
Career(s):
Education:
Unique Skillset:

MOTHER'S MATERNAL GRANDMOTHER
Career(s):
Education:
Unique Skillset:

FATHER'S FATHER
Career(s):
Education:
Unique Skillset:

FATHER'S MOTHER
Career(s):
Education:
Unique Skillset:

MOTHER'S FATHER
Career(s):
Education:
Unique Skillset:

MOTHER'S MOTHER
Career(s):
Education:
Unique Skillset:

FATHER
Career(s):
Education:
Unique Skillset:

MOTHER
Career(s):
Education:
Unique Skillset:

ME
Career(s):
Education:
Unique Skillset:

Porscha Jackson ©

REFERENCES

Alliman-Brissett, A., Turner, S., & Skovholt, T. (2004). Parent support and African American adolescents' career self-efficacy. Professional School Counseling, 7(3), 124-132.

Beeth, H. & Wintz, C.D. (1992). Black Dixie: Afro-Texan history and culture in Houston. College Station, TX: Texas A&M University Press.

Besemer, S. & Farrington, D. (2012). Intergenerational transmission of criminal behavior: Conviction trajectories of fathers and their children. European Journal of Criminology, 9(2), 120-141.

Blackwelder, J.K. (2003). Styling Jim Crow: African American beauty training during segregation. College Station, TX: Texas A&M University Press.

Chavarria, H. (1989, April 27). Hispanics bring rich history to the area. Bryan-College Station Eagle, 13(e).

Chope, R. (2006). Family Matters: The influence of the family in career decision making. Austin, TX: Pro Ed.

Dippel, Jr. T. (2002). The new legacy. Brenham, TX: Texas Peacemaker Publications, LLC.

Eagle. (1974, January 20).

Eaton, C. (2012, September 7). Baylor to honor two Houston family businesses. Houston Business Journal. Retrieved from http://www.bizjournals.com/houston/news/2012/09/07/baylor-to-honor-texas-familybusiness.html

Fingerman, K., Sechrist, J. & Birditt, K. (2013). Changing views on intergenerational Ties. Gerontology, 59, 64-70.

Frazier, S. (2012). The man who brought a mountain of soul to Houston. Trafford Publishing.

Fulcher, M. (2011). Individual differences in children's occupational aspirations as a function of parental traditionality. Sex Roles, 64, 117-131.

Galagan, J. (1985). Psychoeducational testing: Turn out the lights, party's over. Exceptional Children, 52, 288-299.

Hargrove, B., Creagh, M., & Burgess, B. (2002). Family interaction patterns as predictors of vocational identity and career decision-making self-efficacy. Journal of Vocational Behavior, 61, 185-201.

Hargrove, B., Inman, A., & Crane, R. (2005). Family interaction patterns, career planning attitudes, and vocational identity of high school adolescents. Journal of Career Development, 31(4), 263-278.

Jackson, P. R. (2016). A tale of two legacies: Career narratives of the Black Family Business. Journal of Black Studies, 47(1), 53-72.

Jackson, P.R. (2014). Family careers reloaded: Lessons for the 21st century workforce (Doctoral dissertation, Texas A&M University). Retrieved: http://oaktrust.library.tamu.edu/handle/1969.1/153953

Lewis, T. (2011). Assessing social identity and collective efficacy as theories of group motivation at work. The International Journal of Human Resource Management, 22 (4), 963-980.

Livingston, J. (2009, October 16). Citizen of the year: Rebeca Romero Rainey. The Taos News. Retrieved from http://taosnews.com/news/article_d0ead6dd-050a-510e-b72a-4cead282bfbb.html?mode=print

Logan, J.R. (2011, April 7). Town of Taos hires lawyer to pursue land grant suit. The Taos News. Retrieved from http://www.taosnews.com/news/article_763017bc-ecc4-5bcb-88f5-e255b55f5062.html?mode=print

Maroon Weekly. (2014, March 4). Casa Rodriguez. Retrieved from http://maroonweekly.com/casa-rodriguez-2

McAdams, D., Hart, H. & Maruna, S. (1998). The anatomy of generativity. In D. McAdams & E. St. Aubin (Eds.), Generativity and adult development: How and why we care for the next generation, (pp.7-43). Washington, DC: American Psychological Association.
    Mosely, E. (2015, July 6). Incarcerated-children of parents in prison impacted. Retrieved from https://www.tdcj.state.tx.us/gokids/gokids_articles_children_impacted.html

Seibert, S., Kraimer, M. & Liden, R. (2001). A social capital theory of career success. Academy of Management Journal, 44(2), 219-237.

Smith, C.L. (2011). Family and role model influence on Black young adults' dysfunctional career thoughts (Doctoral dissertation, Regent University). Available from ProQuest Dissertations and Theses database. (UMI No. 3492435).

Solomon, A., Breunlin, D., Gustafson, M., Ransburg, D., Ryan, C., Hammerman, T., & Terrien, J. (2011). "Don't lock me out": Life-story interviews of family business owners facing succession. Family Process, 50(2), 149-166.

Stringer, K. & Kerpelman, J. (2010). Identity development in college students: Decision making, parental support, & work experience. International Journal of Theory & Research, 10(3), 181-200.

Whiston, S. & Keller, B. (2004). The influences of the family or origin on career development: A review and analysis. The Counseling Psychologist, 32(4), 493-568.

AFTERWORD

Well, let me just say thank you for your interest in this book. This has been a journey for me and now whether you know it or not, you are a part of my life. Yes, we are connected. I hope this connection doesn't end here but continues to grow. I would love to hear how any part of this book has helped you and how you are faring in pursuit of your legacy. I would MOST positively want to hear from those of you who are already part of a family career legacy. There are so many of you out there and your stories need to be heard. I get inspired from your stories, so I know others will be blessed from them as well. You will find my contact information at the end of this afterword. Don't be shy! Remember, we're connected now, so don't disconnect.

Speaking of sharing, I hope you found this book interesting and useful and I hope you will share this with others. I believe we, as individuals, desperately need to hone into our passions and God-given talents and do the work we are destined to perform. We need each other and if we don't live up to our potential we are doing ourselves and the world a disservice. God is so great and has given each of us a purpose, so it would be an insult to the creator to not pursue excellence in our job, career, family, and community. We all can make an impact in our own special way and in doing so, we change the world individually and collectively. Legacy is ours!

I count it as an honor to have entered into the pristine history of the families who shared their career stories and family history. There was so much information they shared; however, I could not tell it all but I did my best in giving you the golden nuggets. In narrating their stories, I started my pursuit to legacy. When I started this research over three years ago, I had no idea what it would lead to; however, in interviewing the families and discovering how open they were to share their stories and for some to voluntarily give me books they had authored to help me better understand their legacy and persona, I was humbled. Ironically, now I have written a book about them and in doing so have started pursuing my legacy. Again, I am so grateful to them.

Pursuing Legacy

This has been such a great accomplishment for me to get this information to you in this format. Like I said in the conclusion, this book only scratches the surface, so look for more to come from me. As I write, I have more things to share with you and am planning fun yet informative ways to bring a greater understanding of legacy to you and the world. You know in graduate school, they told me 'your dissertation is your life's journey' and it has rung true for me. Legacy is so important and I am so passionate about it that I am finding multiple ways to help others in their pursuit of it. I'm not for sure where this path will take me but if I can just help one person, the journey is worth it.

In closing, keep in touch with me at the following social media outlets.

Sincerely blessed,

Porscha R. Jackson, PhD

Email: pursuinglegacy@gmail.com
Website: www.pursuinglegacy.webs.com
Blog: careerlegacy.wordpress.com
Twitter: @successfulshoes
Linked In: porschaj

P.S. Please visit the above website and let me know if you would like any of the featured figures, tables, or worksheets in the book in larger print.

ABOUT THE AUTHOR

Porscha R. Jackson, PhD is an adult educator, certified career coach, philanthropist, and author with a passion for "making people better". She has spent more than 10 years in the nonprofit sector educating, counseling, training, and developing adults for career advancement, community leadership, and scholastic achievement. Throughout her career, she has received awards for her work in the community and is highly recognized and respected for her professionalism, project management accomplishments, and presentations on career-related issues and personnel development. During her doctoral candidacy in human resource development, she developed an interest in the familial influence on careers and has since become a field expert in the research of career legacies and its parallelism to workforce development. Recently, Dr. PJ, as she is affectionately referred to because of her personable approach, has started her own consultancy specializing in career development services. Additionally, she is actively involved in various community and professional organizations centered on human resource development, adult learning, and urban education. She also enjoys advocating for Successful Shoes, a 501 (c) 3 nonprofit organization she founded to provide encouragement through shoe donations and career development services to women in transitional programs and homes.